'This book is a guide to both setting up a practice and cultivating a personal and professional life that is both rewarding and sustainable. It offers insights, pragmatic advice and essential knowledge whilst encouraging you to shape your own ideas via reflective exercises so you can develop a practice that's the right fit for you and your clients. A practice that is consistent with your values and ethics and puts wellbeing, both your own and other people's, at its core. With this book as your guide, you will be well-equipped to create a private practice that resonates with your values, nurtures your wellbeing and fulfils your professional aspirations.'

Dr Mary Welford, *Consultant Clinical Psychologist.*

'Many therapists aspire to set up in private practice yet struggle with where to begin. Written by someone who has been there, done it, and got the T-shirt, this book has you covered. Practical, accessible and personable.'

Jason Roscoe, *CBT Therapist, Trainer, and*
Supervisor in Private Practice

'This is a refreshing and delightful book on private practice by CBT therapist Sarah D. Rees (with contributions from Sophie A. Wood). It provides the much needed 'bog standard' information for those looking to set up in private practice – finance and tax; marketing and branding, as well as providing a clear and empathic understanding of some of the challenges a therapist may face, such as, moving from full employment to private practice. What I most like about this book is how accessible it is. The chapters feature advised-based content, which includes accurate step-by-step instructions on creating a website, as well as useful exercises aimed at helping the reader make clear decisions, in their goal to establish a values-based practice. Sarah and I share an interest in the power of community-based support for private practitioners, and it is a pleasure to recommend this book.'

Caz Binstead *is an integrative therapist, and specialist*
in private practice. She was the divisional lead
(and architect) of the BACP Private practice toolkit,
is a published writer (and author), and,
co-lead of #TherapistsConnect.

'A timely and warmly written book that will be useful for counselling and psychotherapy students, educators, and supervisors working with supervisees in private practice. Sarah shares the valuable lessons she has learnt whilst working in private practice throughout the book in the hope that the reader can navigate a smoother path.'

Elaine Beaumont, *Lecturer and Psychotherapist at*
School of Health & Society, University of Salford.

'This is the book I wish I'd had when I began my private practice; but it's also the book I'm excited to finally have, 10 years later! Answering all the common 'what if' questions that therapists consistently raise regarding independent work, and providing lots of practical advice and reassurance, this is a must-have for any therapists practicing, or considering practicing, within the private sphere. Not only will it help you to establish and build an effective and successful therapy practice, it will also encourage you to consider how to do this in a way that aligns with your values and satisfies you both financially and professionally.'

Dr Hannah Wilson, *Clinical Psychologist*

A Therapist's Guide to Private Practice

This book is a comprehensive guide to setting up, running and growing a successful private therapy practice that resonates with your values and professional goals.

Guiding you through every detail, from making the initial decision to set up your own private therapy practice to scaling your practice, this guide will support you in overcoming the common challenges you may encounter. It is filled with practical exercises, templates and checklists, including business planning actions at the end of each chapter so you can craft your first business plan. Ensuring you have a solid foundation and can shape a private therapy practice that meets your financial and personal needs while reflecting the passion that led you to your profession.

A motivational and inspiring read for therapists, psychotherapists, coaches, and counsellors. Get ready to turn your dream into reality and create something profoundly impactful and uniquely yours.

Sarah D. Rees is a CBT Therapist with a successful private practice in Cheshire. She founded the popular Substack community, 'Therapists Corner,' which has supported thousands of therapists to set up and grow their private practice. She is passionate about high-quality, diverse mental health provision being developed in a way that is valued and accessible.

Sophie A. Wood is a website and graphic designer with 25 years of Information Technology and security expertise. Sophie founded Pocket Site in 2017 – a website builder tailored for healthcare professionals. Sophie is dedicated to demystifying the internet through a range of tools and resources she has created, such as the Therapist Fee Calculator and GDPR resources, to empower professionals in the digital age, enabling them to concentrate on delivering impactful therapy by simplifying the business side of their practice.

A Therapist's Guide to Private Practice

Practice

Building a Values-based Business

Sarah D. Rees

with contributions by Sophie A. Wood

Routledge
Taylor & Francis Group

LONDON AND NEW YORK

Designed cover image: Photograph by Jessica Howell

First published 2025
by Routledge
4 Park Square, Milton Park, Abingdon, Oxon OX14 4RN

and by Routledge
605 Third Avenue, New York, NY 10158

Routledge is an imprint of the Taylor & Francis Group, an informa business

British Library Cataloguing-in-Publication Data
A catalogue record for this book is available from the British Library

Library of Congress Cataloging-in-Publication Data
Names: Rees, Sarah D., author.
Title: A therapist's guide to private practice : building a
   values-based business / Sarah D. Rees ; with contributions by
   Sophie A. Wood.
Description: Abington, Oxon ; New York, NY : Routledge, 2025. |
   Includes bibliographical references and index.
Identifiers: LCCN 2024015683 | ISBN 9781032512570 (hardback) |
   ISBN 9781032512563 (paperback) | ISBN 9781003401391
   (ebook)
Subjects: MESH: Psychotherapy—organization & administration |
   Private Practice—organization & administration | Practice
   Management, Medical—organization & administration |
   Value-Based Health Care—organization & administration
Classification: LCC RC440.8 .R44 2025 | NLM WM 21 |
   DDC 616.89/140068—dc23/eng/20240430
LC record available at https://lccn.loc.gov/2024015683

ISBN: 978-1-032-51257-0 (hbk)
ISBN: 978-1-032-51256-3 (pbk)
ISBN: 978-1-003-40139-1 (ebk)

DOI: 10.4324/9781003401391

Typeset in Times New Roman
by Apex CoVantage, LLC

Contents

Acknowledgements

I want to extend my love and gratitude to some of the exceptional individuals whose belief in me and my work is an invaluable motivator. Your unwavering support has been deeply appreciated.

To Sophie, Mary, Lisa, Jo, Kirsten, Gayle, Elaine and Graham, your regular check-ins, friendship and shared laughter enrich my life in countless ways. Your presence is always a constant source of strength, whether near or far.

Sophie, Lisa, Mary and Franky, thank you for your hours reading over, checking, moulding and sculpting my words and each motivational nudge. I needed every one. We've brought this book to life for all the amazing therapists out there who are doing exceptional things and will play an important part in developing the landscape of mental health and therapeutic delivery. I can't thank you enough!

To all my clients, who allow me into their worlds and minds through their courage and trust, they continue to teach me invaluable lessons about resilience and the human spirit. Your stories and strength inspire me every single day, I'm truly honoured.

And, of course, for every therapist who dedicates their life to learning and supporting others, your commitment to creating a more compassionate and understanding world is inspiring and nothing short of remarkable.

I greatly appreciate you all and countless others who have influenced and inspired me along the way.

Thank you.

Sarah

Foreword

Like many of you reading this, I remember being aware of psychological distress from an early age and have been motivated to alleviate it ever since. This led to my training as a therapist and subsequent contact with so many amazing clients and colleagues. I've been lucky to have worked with and navigated many different services and specialities throughout my career. I've worked with and for our beloved NHS, some amazing charities, schools and private sector organisations. In my fifth decade, I entered the rich and diverse space of private practice, leading me to work in new areas I hadn't even considered before as a therapist. Throughout this time, with considerable regularity, my path crossed with the amazing Sarah D. Rees. We saw each other at training events and social gatherings and liaised with respect to our clinical work. I was always struck by her warmth, her sense of humour and her knack of being both incredibly down-to-earth and inspirational. She calls a spade a spade and also manages to bring our work to new audiences via blogs, podcasts and downloadable materials. Not content with all of that, she has also produced helpful resources for us therapists too. When Sarah first shared her idea of writing this book, I wholeheartedly encouraged her. It seemed that no sooner had she conceived the idea, the book was being written, and I am now delighted to introduce her practical guide to private practice. When I embarked on my own journey into private practice, resources like this were limited; I kind of bumped myself along, somehow carving a path that was less proactive and more reactive to everyday opportunities and challenges. I would have benefited from a book such as this. This book is a guide to both setting up a practice and cultivating a personal and professional life that is both rewarding and sustainable. It offers insights, pragmatic advice and essential knowledge whilst encouraging you to shape your own ideas via reflective exercises so you can develop a practice that's the right fit for you and your clients. A practice that is consistent with your values and ethics and puts well-being, both your own and other people's, at its core. With this book as your guide, you will be well-equipped to create a private practice that resonates with your values, nurtures your well-being and fulfils your professional aspirations.

Dr Mary Welford
Consultant Clinical Psychologists

Introduction

Congratulations on taking the first step towards setting up your own private therapy practice! I'm thrilled to be a part of this journey with you. I know it can feel overwhelming, but trust me, it's a pivotal moment and will be worth it.

You might be asking yourself:

- Is this the right decision for me?
- Where do I start?
- Will it work out?
- How do I find clients?
- Will I be able to earn enough? The list goes on . . .

Don't worry. This book has you covered. It is the complete step-by-step guide to building and growing a private therapy practice, taking you from the initial decision all the way through to running a successful, sustainable, resilient business aligned with your values and lifestyle.

This is for you if you're a therapist ready to step into private practice confidently. If you are keen to learn from someone who's been gone before you, made mistakes and taken detours but ultimately thrived in private practice, I'm here to guide you on utilising your invaluable therapist skills and expertise to build a practice rooted in your values.

A sustainable, resilient practice that genuinely makes a difference in the world. We'll create a private practice where you can genuinely take pride.

My Journey

My career started in the 1990s. The Care in the Community Act was just taking effect. I was working as a support worker for Social Services, where I helped resettle people with learning needs and mental health problems from the long-outdated Victorian 'asylums' into local communities. I later trained as a mental health nurse, and over time, I grew to think that there was more to recovery than just the medical model of treatment for people. I wanted to find out more about the different psychological approaches, starting with person-centred counselling and later completing

DOI: 10.4324/9781003401391-1

a degree in psychosocial models, where I learned about Cognitive Behavioural Therapy (CBT) and its solid evidence base.

In the mid-2000s, the government in the UK committed to spending £170 million to support the expansion of psychological therapies to provide better support for people with mental health problems. Given this promise for better mental health services, I decided to move, from a management position I was in at the time, back into a clinical role and to undertake the training to become a cognitive behavioural therapist as part of the IAPT (Improving Access to Psychological Therapies) programme. I felt like I was part of something innovative and exciting; there was a real sense that things were finally about to change for the better in the world of mental health care.

After working in the IAPT service for about a year, I began considering what a private practice would look like, mainly due to my frustration at clients' long waiting times. For months, I debated whether I should leave the NHS or not. Eventually, I compromised and reduced my hours to three days a week, leaving me with two full days to focus on developing a private practice.

I found a therapy room and set up my first website with the help of my partner, Sophie (whom you will hear from later in the book). I also joined every health insurance company and referral agency I could, made flyers and business cards, which I posted everywhere, and listed myself on a range of business and therapy directories. Then I waited and waited for my first referrals to roll in. This scattergun approach to building a therapy practice was exhausting and uncertain. It took three months for me to get my first self-referring client. Back then, the bulk of my caseload came from referral agencies, but the demand often fluctuated, and this work came with its own challenges, such as low pay rates and additional paperwork.

The Start of My Private Practice

The gradual approach to building my private practice alongside my NHS role meant that I had proof it was working before I made the leap, entirely. I had a name, website and therapy room, and my caseload was building. However, the first few months I was completely in private practice were daunting. I constantly needed to figure out where my next referral would come from. I spent time looking around at what others were doing, comparing and despairing, wondering if I would ever get my private practice to what I perceived others were like. At this time, I received the most supervision and business coaching for that extra support and guidance on my journey.

In the early days, looking around at your competition can be tempting. I recommend limiting this. Instead, put your blinkers on and run your own race. Embracing your individuality, diversity and uniqueness as a person and therapist will be your superpower.

Fast forward ten years and I run a thriving therapy practice in Wilmslow, Cheshire, where I work a couple of days a week, seeing clients in the clinic or online. I have three therapy rooms and rent out the additional rooms to other therapists, creating a lovely community that benefits from referral-sharing. I have built up several income streams alongside seeing clients on a one-on-one basis, which allows me to earn far more than I would do just seeing clients, and it allows me to support people in various ways while providing me with additional income and, in turn, the flexibility to work at a slower pace. I have earned more than I expected consistently over the last decade and love being able to structure my days and weeks in a way that works best for me and my family. The hard work and uncertainty at the start of setting up in private practice really does pay off.

What This Book Covers

Along with providing a comprehensive overview of the practical step-by-step considerations required for setting up a private practice, there will be exercises and questions for you to answer or reflect on as you go through the book.

This will help you to apply the concepts and information you are reading to your own experiences or circumstances, making the material more meaningful and relevant to you and your context, facilitating reflection self-discovery and helping you identify the areas where you may need additional support or guidance.

At the end of each chapter, there are business planning actions for you to consider. I recommend you complete these as you go through the book because I also want you to have something practical and useful for your business going forward. Completing these actions will give you lots of knowledge about running a private practice, and in the process, you will have also created your first business plan. If there is one thing I wish I had spent more time on at the very start, that would have been planning and creating a business plan. A business plan is a dynamic and evolving document that's constantly growing, much like a formulation in therapy. You don't need to have all the details figured out from the very beginning; instead, the plan should evolve alongside your business.

However, the more comprehensive and well-informed your plan is at each stage, the stronger the foundation you'll have to build upon and grow your business.

In therapy, we start the process by building and developing a comprehensive assessment of each client. A high-quality and considered clinical assessment equips you to create the most effective treatment plan and roadmap for therapy. A business plan plays a very similar role; you learn about your business and develop a roadmap. The better the input, the better the output.

Throughout the book, we'll delve into the common mindset blocks new business owners encounter, and I'll guide you in exploring, challenging and reframing these blocks so they can support your progress. Moreover, I'll equip you with practical strategies to apply your skills as a therapist to your business confidently, reducing any overwhelm you may experience.

This is the book I would have devoured when I set up my private practice in 2014. Back then, it felt like an uncharted path. There were few role models to follow, and information was scarce. I began sharing what I was learning by writing blog posts, coaching therapists in the 'Therapists Corner' community on Substack and delivering workshops, all culminating in this book, which will serve as your mentor and provide the guidance and support you need. The path to building a private practice is hard work, time-consuming and filled with challenges, but I can say from the heart that running my own business on my own terms has been one of the most rewarding things I've ever done and has opened up opportunities I never thought possible.

I am recharged and excited for each new week. It enables me to structure my time and workload to ensure I can show up for my clients when I am at my best. I deliver therapy without the usual organisational boundaries and with less restrictive protocols and time frames.

I have the space and time to reflect on the therapy I deliver; I've been able to undertake the training, coaching and supervision I choose when I need it. If some of these things motivate you to go into private practice, be assured it's achievable, and I will show you how.

Chapters Overview

In the first chapter, I will walk you through some common fears people have so you can work through them yourself and ensure you are making the right decision. Then, we'll focus on finding your 'why' for your business, which will act as your motivation and carry you through every stage of building your business. Business strategy basics will be introduced so you know how to build a solid foundation in your private practice.

In the second chapter, I will provide an overview of the steps you need to take to create your private practice. The chapter will also support you in establishing your core business values; they will shape every decision and action going forward, acting as a lens through which you filter all your ideas and decisions. With a firm foundation of genuine values, your business becomes more than just a venture and has a true purpose and identity.

In Chapter 3, we explore financial management when running a successful private practice. Firstly, we look at money mindset, then the importance of setting financial goals, creating a solid plan and how to set hourly rates accurately,

Chapter 4 guides readers on effective strategies for generating referrals and establishing a sustainable caseload in their private practice. It addresses common anxieties surrounding referral generation and shares my experience with the 'Scattergun Method' approach.

Chapter 5 explores effective values-based marketing techniques for therapists in private practice to build a caseload of self-referring clients. It emphasises creating a marketing strategy that aligns with the therapist's values and caters to potential clients' needs, advocating marketing from a place of service, aiming to help clients find suitable support and therapists. Niching, crafting tailored content and embracing diversity in marketing efforts are explored.

Chapter 6 highlights the pivotal role of a website in your private practice, outlining essential steps to create an effective site that attracts your ideal clients. It emphasises the significance of selecting a simple domain name and using professional photos to establish a strong first impression.

Chapter 7 delves into the critical realm of data protection and client information safeguarding within therapy practices. As therapists, we must collect only essential data, store it responsibly and disclose it with client consent or as required by law. This chapter will help you understand data protection laws and how to implement processes for compliance, including regular policy reviews ensuring that effective communication with clients about data usage fosters trust and confidence.

Chapter 8 explores all the elements you need in place to get ready to deliver therapy sessions. From crafting an ideal workweek to embracing evolving therapy platforms, how to blend your clinical work with your business role. The key tools you need in place, from organised session diaries to clear contracts, ensure a nurturing client journey from the first moment they enquire about therapy until discharge. What policies you should have in place are covered and much more, preparing therapists and clients for a successful therapy journey.

Chapter 9 explores risk assessment; this chapter offers a foundational overview of risk management focusing on private practice. See it as your starting point, emphasising continuous vigilance, adaptability and foresight. Beyond legalities, we prioritise the safety and well-being of all involved. Navigating the complexities of risk, we spotlight key concerns and guide you in establishing robust processes for your practice. If risk management feels daunting, this chapter offers reassurance. With structured planning and the right support, we guide you towards a secure practice. Approach this introduction to therapeutic risk with clarity and confidence, knowing you're on the right path.

Chapter 10 focuses on the indispensable role of self-care for therapists, shaped by my personal lessons and professional insights. It underscores that our effectiveness extends beyond knowledge; it's rooted in our emotional balance and presence. This chapter isn't just about avoiding burnout; it champions self-care as a duty. By nurturing ourselves, we enhance our service to our clients, embodying the core values of our practice.

Chapter 11 will teach you what it means to scale a private practice. Picture a life of financial prosperity with greater flexibility and freedom. Extending your skills and expertise outside of the therapy room so you can support more people. This broadened scope allows for a more impactful dissemination of mental health treatment and expertise. We'll discuss the varied ways clients seek mental health support and how to cater to these needs. The chapter offers a roadmap to firm up your business foundation, ensuring it's primed for growth. We detail strategies from effectively engaging with your audience and mastering email lists to crafting persuasive lead magnets. Furthermore, discover diverse income paths perfect for therapists in private practice.

At the end of each chapter, you'll find a business plan action for you to work through. Collating all the information from answering these questions will provide you with your first business plan and a solid foundational platform.

By the end of this book, you will have all the tools you need to confidently set up and successfully build, grow and run a profitable, sustainable therapy business. You already have many skills, expertise and knowledge; this book will show you how to use and apply them to create a private practice with values and purpose and a business and life you love.

Chapter 1

Is Now the Right Time to Start in Private Practice?

Let me assure you, the demand for mental health services shows no signs of slowing down, so the answer is a resounding yes! Now is a great time to take the plunge and set up your own practice. Don't let the fear of timing keep you from pursuing your passion and helping others.

The stigma around mental health and accessing psychological treatment has reduced significantly over recent years. This trend will no doubt continue, with more people looking for support for their mental health. I have noticed a steady increase in clients seeking therapy each year I've been in private practice. I've also seen people no longer reserving therapy for times of crisis but using it as a proactive way to invest in their well-being. People recognise the value of therapy and self-awareness now more than ever and understand how it can empower them to manage their lives and mental health better.

In my previous experience working in the NHS, clients having therapy were entitled to a certain number of therapy sessions, usually eight. However, this one-size-fits-all approach only sometimes meets the needs of individual clients. Some people benefit from having fewer sessions, while others might need more. Unfortunately, I worked with many clients who had to end treatment at an important stage due to the predetermined session limit. In private practice, we can negotiate the number of sessions with each client on a case-by-case basis, allowing treatment to be truly tailored to the individual rather than being constrained by a fixed entitlement.

Finally, there is a significant gap between the need for mental health treatment and its availability. This gap is a global issue, as highlighted by the Mental Health Action Plan 2013–2020, which states that 'the gap between the need for treatment and its provision is large all over the world.' By adapting our approach and meeting our client's specific needs, we can help bridge this gap and ensure more people can access the care they need. Between 76% and 85% of people with severe mental disorders in low-income and middle-income countries receive no treatment at all. The corresponding range for high-income countries is between 35% and 50%. WHO's Mental Health Atlas (2011) provides data demonstrating the scarcity of resources within countries to meet mental health needs and underlines the inequitable distribution and inefficient use of such resources. Globally, spending on mental health

DOI: 10.4324/9781003401391-2

is less than US$2 per person. This demonstrates that it has never been a better time to be a therapist considering private practice: you can make a significant impact. Where there are challenges, there are also opportunities, so these are exciting times, and you are perfectly placed to have the chance to evolve and shape mental health care provision in today's world. Understandably, starting a new venture is full of apprehension and fears, so let's explore this now.

The Fears that Hold Us Back

As therapists, we know all too well about the importance of mindset work for others, but are you aware of your own mindset blocks?

Fears and worries always show up when we are starting something new, and they show up in the form of stubborn mindset blocks, which can hold us back if we don't become aware of them and tackle them. Just like you would work in therapy with your clients to uncover and tackle blocks, it's important to work on your own mindset and start getting to know and address any worries or fears you have as early on as possible so you can overcome the obstacles they present and continue to make progress.

We support our clients to build lives from a safe, secure base, and we need to do the same for our business. Knowing your fears when setting up your business will enable you to plan and support yourself so you don't build a business from a place of fear, which is not a nice place to work and can affect how you run your business. As you grow and evolve with your business, the range of fears and worries shift and change, too, and this is okay; it's all part of the process. One way to deal with these fears is to regularly return to an exercise that helps you identify them and work through them. This might be a journaling practice, a visualisation exercise or something else that works for you. Remember, it's normal as you navigate the ups and downs of private practice, but with a little self-care and a toolkit of strategies, you can work through these as you set up and continue growing your practice confidently.

Exercise

- Take some time to consider your fears about setting up and running a private practice.

  It might be helpful to visualise yourself in the day-to-day operations of your business – seeing clients, managing social media and your website, communicating with your accountant, preparing client files and getting ready for therapy sessions. As you do this, pay attention to where anxiety or fear arises.

- What are the specific aspects of running a private practice that most concern you?

- Ask yourself, what would I be doing if I had no fear? What would my business look like?
- Write out a list of all the fears that come up.
- Then put your therapist hat on and work through the following questions.

For Each Fear, Consider

- Can I break down the steps to make them more achievable?
- Is this fear a fact or an opinion?
- Are these real worries I can plan for or hypothetical?
- Can I put a plan B in place for these fears?
- What steps can I take to increase my support?
- If a colleague or peer expressed these fears and concerns to me, how would I suggest they address them?

Do I Have the Skills to Set Up a Private Practice?

Have you ever worried that you don't have the skills to succeed in private practice? If so, I have some good news: you are more than qualified! As Kathy Ireland said in 2004, 'In business, it's about people. It's about relationships.' As a therapist, you have valuable expertise in building and maintaining those very relationships, a crucial business skill.

Don't let self-doubt hold you back from pursuing your dream of starting your own practice. One of the most important aspects of running a business is building and maintaining relationships, and as a therapist, you excel in this area. For example, the branding and marketing process is all about building relationships with potential clients who just don't know you yet or know that you are the right therapist for them. Building good relationships is also where many opportunities will come from. We are working in a globally digital age, so endless possibilities exist. You can work with people to support your business from all over the world. Good relationships with your accountant and referral sources are the key to a solid private practice and to creating financial security; working well with your website designer will be the relationship that sets you apart from the digital hordes.

Strong relationships make everything easier and will support you in getting your business through tough times. Most recently, when the pandemic hit, my caseload was reduced to a quarter in the first week as people understandably put their therapy on hold so we could collectively and globally figure out what was happening.

Being self-employed and still having my bills to pay, this was unexpected and scary. But I had a safety net, an email list, which is a list of people who have signed up to hear from you on a regular basis. I write a weekly email providing mental health tips and advice. It's where I share blogs and podcasts. People enjoy receiving the emails, and over time, it builds what is known in marketing as the 'Know-Like-Trust factor.' We will talk more about all this in later chapters.

For years, I'd been building this list of people I email weekly with useful content, establishing an effective way of communicating what was happening in my business. This meant that when the pandemic hit, I could reach out and let them know I was available to offer online therapy sessions. Many of them did reach out because they really needed the support at the time. These relationships I had built over the years kept me in business during the pandemic. The people on my email list already knew my work and trusted me; my weekly emails had also kept me at the front of their minds.

By focusing energy and resources on relationships and cultivating a mindset of being of service to people, you can establish connections that work well for you and others, creating a solid network. If you have ever had a concern that private practice can be isolating, I hope I've put pay to that. I have never been so connected with others in my career.

Making the Decision

One thing that helped me leave the NHS was seeing the increasingly high demand for therapists, so if setting up in private practice didn't work out, there would be the option to return to paid employment. Having a plan B was crucial in giving me the security to move forward with my private practice. Financial security, like a few months' salary in the bank, would have also been useful and given me the confidence to say no to some referrals that were not right for me in the early days.

What you need to make the decision may look different, but making that important first decision is your first hurdle. One way is to create a pros-and-cons list, which will allow you to weigh the benefits and drawbacks of private practice, making it easier to determine if it's the right choice. Moya (2024) talks about portfolio working, where therapists have a number of different posts she discusses:

> Adopting the mindset of a CBT entrepreneur allows freedom to think creatively and be flexible in the development of your business. Portfolio working provides a model for building your professional identity in line with your strengths, values, and passions so you can achieve more of the items on your CBT career bucket list and maintain a fulfilling career.

Private practice does come with uncertainty in the early days as it is new territory. Financial insecurity is a certainty, as the steady stream of client referrals takes time to foster. You can safeguard yourself by having a financial buffer, which is an excellent idea at every stage of your business lifespan. In the first few years of private practice, there will also be many hours of unpaid work before it begins to pay off. When you are in paid employment, you know your monthly salary and have a range of protections around sickness, pensions and healthcare. These are a few considerations when deciding whether now is the right time to jump into private practice or whether you need to wait. If now is not the right time, you can put it to one side for a while, or start slowly planning it out and creating your vision so you will have a head start when the time is right.

I've put some questions together for you to consider if you are still at the deciding point. They will be helpful to go through because the more clarity you have about why you are going into private practice, the better.

Is Private Practice Right for Me?

- Why am I considering private practice?
- Why is this important to me?
- Do I have time to commit to this every week for planning and preparing?
- How will I feel if I decide not to venture into private practice?
- What are the risks, and how can I manage them?
- What will my business and life look like if private practice works well?

Running a private therapy practice is hard work. It's certainly not an easy option, so clarity on why you chose this path is important and will give you regular injections of motivation.

Once you have made the decision, it's time to make it a reality, which is scary. I began by deciding on a date when I would hand in my notice to terminate my employment. I wrote it in bold in my diary.

"On 1st August 2014. I will hand in my notice and run my own private therapy practice."

If this is where you are, I want you to decide on a date now when you will either leave your current position to start your private practice or the date you will begin to set up your private practice. Write it in your diary or on a sticky note where you will see it daily.

On date . . . month . . . year . . . I will set up my private therapy practice and run my own business. I will be a business owner.

When you have the clarity of the date, you can begin to step into the reality of it, start your research and planning and start carving out your path.

In CBT, we encourage our clients to write things out because it makes it real when it's out of their heads and down on paper. It gives you more clarity and a new perspective.

Initially, I struggled with even the thought of being a business owner. The title alone was out of my comfort zone. Arriving at my desk and opening my diary to see it written down every day helped me adjust to the reality of my new career path and let the emotion of fear and overwhelm settle. When you read it and say to yourself enough times, 'I'm a business owner,' or 'I run my own private practice,' you begin to grow into your new title and own it. It becomes normal and just how it is. Instead of being caught up in the title, you can focus on the work you need to do.

I'd also recommend telling a few people. People who have your back, believe in you and are your biggest supporters. They will help you believe in yourself, help you maintain momentum and keep you accountable. I can be a bit of an open book and get overexcited, so my reality was that I told lots of people. Some people were judgemental and critical of my choice or became a little competitive, so telling everyone was not the best idea. We focus on negatives much more than the positives, and having this unnecessary negative noise around you is just not helpful. You are now a business owner and an important asset; looking after yourself and surrounding yourself with compassionate supporters is important.

You have made the decision and nailed down a date. The next thing you will see is a looming mountain of everything you have to do. This can feel overwhelming. I'm sure many prospective business owners have shut up shop at this point. In my coaching sessions with therapists, I always tell them to focus on the small steps before them rather than on the mountain. This is where I want you to spend most of your time – working on the next step in front of you.

Finding Your Why

Your first steps are more about your mindset than the practicalities. You have made the decision, you have worked on your fears, and you are still reading, so private practice is the right step for you.

Next up is finding your 'why.' Why is this so important to you? What will it provide for your career? Why do you want to deliver therapy in this way? Your 'why' is also your mission statement.

> German philosopher Frederick Nietzsche once said, 'He who has a why can endure any how.'

A strong 'why' in business is paramount, particularly in crafting a values-aligned private practice. It offers purpose and direction and guides your decisions. This clear sense of purpose inspires collaboration and helps distinguish your business in a competitive market. More than just profit, a compelling 'why' fosters client trust. Your 'why' is vital during challenges, linking you to your motivation and shining through in your business messaging. Drawing from Simon Sinek's insights, people resonate with your 'why' over what you do. Watching his TED Talk is illuminating; many top brands owe their success to a defined 'why' or mission.

> *People don't buy what you do, they buy why you do it.*
> Simon Sinek (2009)

WHY, HOW, WHAT

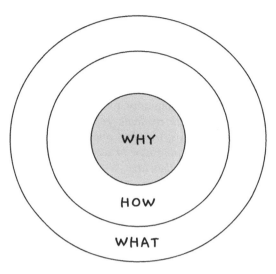

Figure 1.1 The golden circle.

According to Sinek, the fundamental difference between brands that succeed and brands that fail is having a strong 'why' and using it as a starting point for all marketing efforts. To explain this concept, Sinek has developed what he calls the 'Golden Circle' (Figure 1.1).

- Why – This is the core belief of the business. It's *why* the business exists.
- How – This is *how* the business fulfils that core belief.
- What – This is *what* the company does to fulfil that core belief.

Sinek found that most companies do their marketing backwards. They start with their 'what' and then move to the 'how.' Most of these companies even neglect to mention 'why.' Many of them don't even know why they do what they do!

Let's look at some examples.

- The tech giant Apple has a 'why' of 'bringing the best user experience to its customers through innovative hardware, software and services.' Apple's mission statement is clear, concise and to the point. They are evidently determined to deliver quality products for their clients.
- John Lewis's 'why' is 'working in partnership for a happier world.'
- Tesla's 'why' is 'we're building a world powered by solar energy, running on batteries and transported by electric vehicles.' This allows the company to expand and provide much more than cars in the future.

It took me some time to understand the importance of having a clear mission and knowing my why, but it's now always firmly in my mind and keeps me aligned with my values and steers my private practice accordingly.

- For my private practice, my 'why' is *to make modern, effective mental health care more accessible and deliver it with compassion and professionalism.* My 'how' is *through the modalities of therapy I'm trained in,*' and my 'what' is *delivering one-on-one therapy.*
- For Therapists Corner, our community for therapists, the 'why' is *to bring therapists together to cultivate resilient, rewarding, and value-driven businesses. Through posts, podcasts, training, interactive Q&As, power hours and resources. Therapists are learning how to set up, build and grow their private practice for a business and life they love.*

Understanding your 'why' will help you overcome mindset barriers, align firmly with your values, and market your business authentically in a way that potential clients can connect with. When starting a business, trying to appeal to everyone can be tempting. But trying to appeal to everyone tends to ensure you appeal to no one due to a lack of focus and clarity in your messaging. Many therapist websites have long lists of the types of therapy they can offer and lists of conditions or symptoms they can treat to appeal to everyone and improve their website's visibility. Search engines have advanced significantly and can override this tactic to ensure they align people with the most relevant, useful content for them. These lists are a waste of valuable real estate. The truth is, clients just don't relate to them; they seek a therapist they can trust and connect with. A concise marketing message establishes trust and differentiates you from competitors, making your services memorable.

You might be thinking your 'why' is about making a lot of money, and it's true that starting a private therapy practice could potentially bring in more income. However, if your primary motivation is money, you probably shouldn't have chosen a career in the caring professions, which are renowned for being undervalued and underpaid (hopefully, this will change in the future). Dig deeper to find your 'why' with this exercise:

Write out your career history to date, and reflect on why you made each move. What were your values, motivations or reasons for each step? This can help you better understand your career path and identify patterns or themes in your decision-making.

- Ask yourself at least five times why you do what you do
- Ask a few friends and colleagues why they think you do what you do
- Ask yourself five times why you want to set up a private practice
- When are you at your best at work?
- What have been your career highlights so far?

- What are the moments that light you up?
- What are your work values?

Go through your notes and make a list of common themes or words. Rank them in order of importance, with the most important at the top. Your top 5 themes are your 'why.'

From the themes you have identified, write out your 'why' statement here:

_____
_____
_____
_____
_____
_____
_____
_____
_____
_____
_____
_____

If you get stuck, ask a friend, supervisor, coach or colleague who can objectively read through your notes and consider what stands out for them. Sometimes, we can be too close to things to see common themes and values. I worked with a business coach when developing my 'why,' and I initially came up with five keywords:

- Accessibility
- Effectiveness
- Modern
- Professional
- Compassionate

Based on these, I then created my 'why' statement:

> *To make modern, effective mental health care more accessible and deliver it with compassion and professionalism.*

For Therapists Corner, the statement is:

> *Connecting therapists to foster resilient, value-driven practices. Through diverse resources and engagement, we empower therapists to build a thriving private practice they're passionate about.*

Draft your 'why' statement and display it where you'll see it daily. You'll remain aligned with your business mission by consistently reminding yourself of your values and motivations.

Let Your 'Why' Guide You

My 'why' drives my business. After years in the NHS with its prolonged waiting lists, I saw the need for timely mental health support in private practice. I've extended my reach through blogs and podcasts for those unable to access immediate help. Every aspect of my business, from design to branding, mirrors this 'why.' I wrote this book recognising a knowledge gap for therapists in or considering private practice. Remember, when challenges build, your 'why' propels you forward; it's the beacon that illuminates your path.

Conclusion

In this chapter, you've discovered that now is the perfect time to launch your private practice. There's less stigma and a growing appreciation for mental health and self-awareness, with many seeking tailored therapeutic experiences over generic solutions.

Launching a business naturally brings along fears and self-doubt. Yet, addressing these concerns paves the way for a venture you'll truly resonate with. Your foundational skills, especially your adeptness in forging relationships, are invaluable assets in areas like branding and marketing. For those apprehensive about the solitude in private practice, I can attest: It's been the most connective phase of my career.

Private practice demands dedication, requires initial unpaid hours and lacks the fixed income of salaried roles. But in return, it promises unmatched flexibility – empowering you to practice on your terms, chase desired training, and shape your hours around personal needs.

If you're contemplating this path, clarity in your 'why' is indispensable. This guiding star will navigate you through challenges and keep your spirit ignited. Once committed, cement a commencement date. Yes, it's intimidating, but concentrating on immediate tasks rather than the extensive checklist can simplify the journey.

Your 'why' is more than just a reason; it's a beacon. It offers direction, aids in genuine marketing and fortifies trust with prospective clients. As one of my mentors and coaches, Amy Porterfield, wisely remarked in 2023, 'You are creating a life and business by your own design and that kind of greatness takes time.' Imprint this 'why' somewhere daily visible. Such clarity doesn't only distinguish you but sustains your commitment during tribulations.

The journey you're embarking on will have lots of ups and downs. That's the nature of running a business. But if you keep facing your fears and making bold decisions, hold on to your reason 'why' and let purpose guide you; you're bound to make it through. You've got this!

Business Plan Actions

Let's get things rolling if you decide to step into private practice! First things first: pick your start date. That's your big leap moment. Next up, dive deep into your 'why.' Grab a pen and jot down that all-important date and your heartfelt 'why' statement here (Figure 1.2).

ACTIONS

THE DATE I WILL SET UP A
PRIVATE THERAPY PRACTICE   ---

MY WHY

Figure 1.2 Business plan action: Write out the date you will start your private practice and your 'why.'

Chapter 2

Your Next Key Decisions

Setting up your private practice will be both exhilarating and daunting. There are many things to consider and steps to take. You know it's what you want to do now, but knowing where to start is tricky, especially if you've never set up a business before.

This chapter takes you through the essential steps of establishing your private practice, firstly by providing a visual overview of each step in the 'Done Diagram' and then exploring each element required to create a successful private practice, from establishing your business strategy, to establishing your value base and mission, to creating a clear vision for your business. We'll then begin to work through some of the initial practicalities of setting up, such as choosing your practice name, identifying your marketplace position and the ideal clients you want your business to serve. Together, each element will provide you with clarity and direction, supporting you in establishing a solid foundation for your new business so you can feel more confident as you head into the next chapter. You'll be well on your way to building a thriving private practice that aligns with your professional goals and personal values. So, let's get started on this exciting adventure together.

Introducing the Done Diagram

The visual shown in Figure 2.1 breaks down the journey you're embarking on into clear, practical steps, giving you an overview of what you need to do along the way. Understanding the strategy and the bigger picture from the outset lets you grasp the trajectory from your current position to your desired destination.

Step 1 – Decide and define. You begin by deciding to go into private practice. You identify and reframe the initial worries and fears that inevitably arise so you can move past them or allow them minimal space on your journey. Then, you focus on your 'why,' enhancing your clarity and motivation. Next, it's time to define what running your own private therapy practice will look like by establishing a clear business strategy outlining your business's values, mission and vision, all of which act as a filter through which you will make all your business decisions. They will be the guides that shape your private practice.

DOI: 10.4324/9781003401391-3

THE PLAN TO GET IT - DONE

Figure 2.1 The Done Diagram.

Step 2 – Set the objectives and organise. With a robust values system in place and a clear business strategy, it's time to begin setting your objectives. An objective is a specific and measurable goal or outcome that a person or business plans to achieve. You will have many as you go along. Consider writing them out as part of your business plan and ticking them off as you go. When you have your list of objectives, it's time to organise them, depending on their priority. Every business is different, so the list of objectives to reach your unique vision will be different, too.

Step 3 – Navigate and network. Navigating your business means taking the necessary actions to guide its direction and growth. Once you are up and running, you will constantly navigate your path. A business is never static. Navigating is about identifying and overcoming challenges and making constant adjustments, even small ones. The aim is to stay on track and align with your business strategy. Navigating your business also involves adapting to changes in the market, technology, economy and client needs. It's about steering your business towards your vision.

Networking is about the relationships you build within your business, such as potential clients you will work with, colleagues you might collaborate with, or referral sources you connect with. Networking activities include attending industry events or conferences, joining professional associations, participating in online forums or social media groups and connecting with people on professional platforms like LinkedIn.

Step 4 – Execute and examine. Once you've got your strategy in place, it's time to take action, execute it and make things happen. Regularly examining and evaluating your progress and readjusting your goals will allow you to expand your vision and stay on track towards achieving your objectives. A business strategy that provides monthly goals and objectives revisited quarterly is the ideal tool to ensure you regularly examine your business. In much the same way, we regularly review our treatment plans for our clients. So, roll up your sleeves and get ready to execute your plans, keeping an eye on the bigger picture as you go!

If you're feeling overwhelmed by all the considerations and the Done Diagram hasn't simplified things for you yet, remember you are in control of the size and growth of your business. If you're starting your practice while also working another job, it's important to have a clear visual overview of the principles. You can then simplify each step to make it manageable alongside other commitments. In fact, this should be one of your objectives. There's no need to rush. You can decide to work on only one of your objectives at a time or break down your larger vision into smaller steps. Think about how you achieve this for your clients. How do you break down their goals into small, achievable steps? We have the skills, but sometimes need a reminder to apply them to ourselves.

Business Strategy

Many business owners overlook strategy in the first instance and set up without a clear business identity, objectives or plan on how to get to their destination; if you don't know where you are going or how, you won't reach your destination.

Generally, when things start to go wrong and you need to return to the drawing board, people realise they need to develop a strategy. This is precisely what happened for me. I initially created a business that I wasn't happy in, working for many different referral companies that didn't align with my values and seeing clients who were not the right fit for me. The first business coach I worked with had the task of teaching me strategy, and I've never looked back.

Often, new business owners dive head first into their new ventures without a guiding strategy or a clear roadmap for their goals. It's like setting out on a journey; without knowing the destination or the route, how can you ever hope to arrive?

This is especially true for therapists because there is no preparation for private practice in our training, and so much out there around business planning and strategy is directed at large corporate organisations, which is difficult to relate to.

At the time of writing, a quick Google search tells me that 20% of businesses fail in the first year and 60% in the first three years. One of the core reasons behind unsuccessful businesses is a lack of planning and strategy (Lussier & Pfeifer, 2001).

McMullin (2022) states, 'Without strong strategic decisions, your customers will feel lost, your products or pitches will feel unfocused and the purpose behind your business will be unclear.' Decision-making is what business strategy is all about. If there are no decisions, there is no strategy. If there's no strategic decision-making, there is no success. Your business won't survive without a strategy.

What Is Strategy?

A business strategy is the identity of your business; it illuminates your current position and pinpoints your desired destination, so it takes you from point A, where you are now, to point Z, where you want to go to, and business planning charts the course to reach it. In essence, a business strategy answers the 'why' and 'what' of your business objectives.

Strategy and planning fit like two pieces of a puzzle; the foundational elements that underpin both are the business's values. Both are dynamic and ever-evolving documents that adapt to business environments and internal operations changes. While the strategy offers a broad, holistic view, business planning offers granularity, ensuring that every aspect of the business works harmoniously towards the strategic goals.

The elements of a business strategy include knowing why you do what you do, which you covered in the previous chapter, which leads to developing the mission for your private practice. Your business mission is why it exists, what it does and who it is for. You then create the vision of what the world will look like when your business has achieved its mission. The business planning actions at the end of this chapter invite you to write out your business strategy. Underpinning every successful business is a comprehensive values system.

Establishing Your Core Business Values

Values are the guiding beliefs and principles determining how you and your business function. They develop through your experiences, upbringing and social and cultural influences. In the previous chapter, you uncovered your 'why,' which is the motivation that drives you forward to create your business mission and vision, which is your business strategy. Underpinning every aspect of your business should be a solid values base. Values in your business act as your guiding beliefs and principles, providing a resilient foundation for all your decisions and actions, serving as a filter for your thoughts, ideas and choices. Typical values include honesty, confidentiality, integrity, respect, compassion and accountability; the values you choose will play a crucial role in shaping your private practice's culture and atmosphere, from how it feels to work there to your clients' first impressions and emotions when they discover your practice and begin working with you.

We are no longer attracted to businesses that just want to make money. We want to be a part of something bigger and exciting. We crave connection and meaning in a world that's often disconnected. When you have a solid values base, your business be more rewarding to be a part of because it has purpose; you will also build something authentic and relatable that others will want to be a part of.

The Queen of Shops, Mary Portas, explains it well in her 2021 book *Rebuild*, which she wrote during the Covid pandemic:

> Over the past thirty years, the business of what we buy has been dominated by the biggest, fastest and cheapest. But those values no longer resonate. We've come to realise that more doesn't equal better. How we live, buy and sell is changing. The post-pandemic era is all about care, respect and understanding the implications of what we're doing. This 'Kindness Economy' is a new value system where in order to thrive, businesses must understand the fundamental role they play in the fabric of our lives. Businesses need to add, not just grow, balancing commerce with social progress. Because we don't just want to buy from brands – we want to buy into them.
>
> (Portas, 2021)

When someone starts the journey of seeking therapy, it is not just about finding any therapist; it's about finding the right one. They're searching for a connection and a trusted space for someone who resonates with their values, offering a haven of understanding, safety and empathy, someone who can walk with them on this journey.

Your business values lay the foundation for such a space. They shape the unique, therapeutic relationship, allowing you to shine authentically. That way, clients who align with your approach can identify you as the perfect fit even before that first session begins; it's a bond that starts forming right from the very first impression.

So, how do you pinpoint these values? Dive deep into your own experiences and beliefs. Reflect on what drives you, what you passionately advocate for, and the principles you hold dear. That's your compass in the therapeutic world.

Ask Yourself

- When clients discover your private practice, how do you want them to feel?
- What do you want to convey in your messaging to your clients?
- Do you hold personal values you want to mirror in your business?
- What are the values your business will hold?

The aim should not be to align with everyone's values, as this is impossible. You can make a bigger impact with your values and ensure broader inclusion when considering how your business and its values fit within the communities our clients live in. You must consider the diversity and broader spectrum of people within each community.

Ask Yourself

- What will your business add to the community it's in?
- How can your business contribute to social progress?
- What will your business stand for?
- What local support could your business provide?

Another way to explore your business values is by reflecting on other brands or organisations you admire.

Try this exercise:

Consider five brands, shops or services you regularly enjoy using.
Now consider five brands, shops or services you would not use.

Knowing what you don't want to be aligned with is as helpful as knowing what you do want to be aligned with.

As therapists, we are generally associated with a professional or regulatory body that sets out professional and ethical standards that we must uphold in our practice. They ensure that we act in a responsible and trustworthy way towards clients. Print off your professional code of conduct and integrate it into your values and private practice business planning.

In today's fast-paced world, it's easy to get caught up in the daily hustle and lose sight of what truly matters. Understanding your business values and writing them down in your business plan will keep them front and centre so they can continue to guide and shape your business.

If you're still struggling, try brainstorming every word that comes to mind when you think about your business. Create a mind map and see where it takes you. Alternatively, journal about parts of your career or jobs you have enjoyed and reasons you have changed roles. What are the values that stand out for you? Clarity around your values can take time. If you don't feel clear, move on to the next step and return to these exercises later.

Taking Action

Once you are clear about your values, it's time to operationalise them. You need to put them into action and make them part of the everyday operations of your business.

Consider

> * What will I do to support those values?
> * How will I demonstrate my practice values to my clients?
> * What are the rewards for acting in line with the value?
> * Are there negatives for not working in line with the values?
> * What is not in line with or supports the business values?
> * How can I keep the values central to the business?
> * How will my evaluation system keep the business aligned with the values?

Establishing and embracing your core values are essential in building a successful private practice. Your values serve as a compass, guiding your actions, decisions and interactions with clients and colleagues. By defining and integrating these values into every aspect of your practice, you'll create a solid foundation for growth, foster meaningful relationships and cultivate a fulfilling professional life that aligns with your personal beliefs and aspirations. As you progress in your private practice journey, remember to stay true to your values to ensure your practice mission and vision genuinely reflect who you are and what you stand for.

Creating a Clear Business Vision

With a strong foundation of values in place and a clear strategy, it's time to look ahead and create a vision for your private practice. Your vision will serve as the guiding star, providing direction and inspiration as you navigate the challenges and opportunities that lie ahead. It will guide your efforts towards achieving your objectives and bringing your mission to life. In this section, we'll explore how to craft a compelling vision that aligns with your values and propels your private practice toward success.

When you start your private practice, you may work harder than you would in a traditional 9–5. It can feel like there is little or no reward. You can mitigate this challenge with a clear vision which is effectively what will be different in the world and your life when your business mission has been achieved.

Visualisation has become a popular and accepted technique in the sporting world. More recently, it has been adopted by therapists and coaches so we can help our clients create positive outcomes or changes in their lives. Visualisation involves building a clear mental image of your goals and/or engaging in mental rehearsal of something you hope to do or get better at, such as building a success-ful private practice. Spend time creating a crisp, vivid mental picture of what you want your therapy practice to become. With this well-defined vision, you will have a clear sense of direction, focus, clarity and motivation.

Visualising your success reduces stress as you have more certainty about what you are creating. It can also help you feel excited and optimistic about what lies ahead. Ultimately, it will add to your confidence as a business owner. When you have a clear vision, it's also easier to communicate it to others, resulting in more effective branding and messaging.

Visualisation Exercise

Start by bringing to mind your 'why' and the mission this has set you on in creating your therapy practice.

1. Start by taking a few minutes to clear your mind and relax.
2. Imagine yourself in the future when your therapy practice is up and running and has achieved its goals.
3. What are you doing? How are you dressed? What is your therapy room like? What is your life like now?
4. Visualise your practice in detail. What does it look and feel like? Are there people working there? What are they doing? Describe the atmosphere.
5. Imagine the clients attending their session. How do they feel? What are they saying about your services?
6. What is different in the world because your business exists?
7. Once you have a clear business image, write down a few sentences describing it. Use descriptive words and phrases that capture the essence of what you have imagined.

8. Finally, use the information from this exercise to create a vision statement or short paragraph describing your business. Be concise and inspiring, and clearly describe what success looks like for you, your clients and your therapy practice.

This exercise will leave you feeling excited, motivated and empowered. Creating your vision will carry you through tough days when referrals are low or things feel out of reach. If you are a visual person, you could create a vision board for your business that includes images, quotes, and other elements that inspire and motivate. You can use magazines and cut out images or download pictures from Pinterest and upload them to a digital vision board template. I have mine as the screensaver on my phone, reminding me daily of the life I'm working towards.

Share your business vision with people you trust and get some feedback. This can help you refine your vision and make it more impactful. Gathering feedback can feel scary, but it's valuable and you will get used to it quickly. If you have a vision, you have a clear direction and can put the strategies and goals in place to make it real. It's not a fixed point either – your vision will constantly change.

In hindsight, I wish I had devoted more time to planning at the outset of my private practice and begun, as Stephen Covey recommends, 'begin with the end in mind' (Covey, 1989). This quote emphasises the importance of setting clear goals and having a vision for what you want to achieve before taking action. After all, how do we know what we are building without a vision? It might feel time-consuming now, but I promise you are saving yourself a lot of time by working on the clarity of your business.

SMART Goals and Tactics

With your business strategy in place and a solidified mission, vision and values, it is time to put the practical steps in place. This means setting precise goals and defining the tactics to achieve them. For therapists, this isn't just about business metrics; it's about ensuring that your professional aspirations align with the impact you wish to have on your clients' lives.

Setting SMART Goals

SMART is an acronym that can guide you in setting clear, actionable goals. It stands for Specific, Measurable, Achievable, Relevant and Time-bound.

Specific: Be clear about what you want to achieve. Instead of 'I want to help more people,' a specific goal would be 'I want to see five new clients each month.'

Measurable: You should be able to track your progress. You could track the number of new enquiries and client intakes for the above goal.

Achievable: Set goals that challenge you but are within reach. Aiming for 20 new clients a month might be unrealistic if you are just starting.

Relevant: Your goals should align with your mission, vision, and values. If your mission emphasises quality therapy, keep that for quantity.

Time-bound: Assign a deadline. 'I want to see five new clients monthly for the next six months.'

Once your SMART goals are in place, it's vital to determine the exact steps to get there.

Increase referrals: If your goal is to gain new clients, tactics include networking with other healthcare professionals, offering workshops or enhancing your online presence through a revamped website or targeted social media ads.

Skill development: For therapists aiming to specialise further, tactics could involve attending specialised training, seeking supervision in that area or joining professional groups focusing on that speciality.

Client retention: Enhancing the therapeutic experience, tactics might involve integrating feedback tools, offering flexible session timings or creating a comforting therapy space.

Operational efficiency: If managing administrative tasks better is a goal, tactics might include investing in therapy-specific software or hiring administrative support.

Continuous feedback: Regularly ask for feedback from clients or peers. This helps refine your tactics and ensures you're on the right path.

With a values-based business strategy at the heart of your private practice, it's then about deciding where to focus your energy and resources to create the most significant impact. Each goal you set and tactic you employ contribute to the tapestry of healing and growth you offer your clients. With a clear 'why,' mission, vision and values, your SMART goals and tactics will drive your practice's success and ensure you remain true to the essence of your business journey, leading to deeper purpose, more fulfilment and often, more success.

Choosing a Business Name

Your first practical decision is to choose the name for your therapy practice. This name will become a potential client's first impression of the business. A good name can help establish a positive image and make it easier for clients to remember you and find you.

When I first started in private practice, I chose the name CheshireCBT.co.uk. I was based in Wilmslow, which is in the county of Cheshire as I am now, and I was keen for my name to reflect a broad area. This tactic was driven by the fear that narrowing the area would reduce my reach and, in turn, reduce referrals. Therefore, I cast my net as wide as possible, not understanding the principles of choosing a name for a business. In reality, it was improbable that anyone would enter 'Cheshire CBT' into a search engine when seeking a therapist. Instead, they are more likely to use search terms such as 'Wilmslow therapy,' 'local therapist near me,' or 'CBT in Wilmslow.'

The problem was that I should have put myself in my client's shoes and considered how they would look for a therapist. I now know the name of your business is not as important as the content you create within the website or on social media platforms. Creating engaging and valuable content is crucial for reaching potential clients and building a successful therapy practice (do not worry – we will cover this in greater depth in Chapter 5).

A few months later, I realised I wasn't the only CBT therapist with this idea. There was already CBTCheshire.co.uk, Cheshirecbtcenter.co.uk and others. This was very confusing for clients. Several people phoned me when they were booked in with another therapist with a similar version of the same name. This wasn't the worst of it. I was getting daily phone calls from people who wanted to book in for their test! I confidently assured them there were no exams or tests to be taken with CBT. However, it turns out they were right because they wanted to book their 'Compulsory Basic Training' (CBT), a course in the UK you have to take before you ride a moped or motorcycle on the road. The lesson from this is that when you choose a name, you first need to type it into a search engine like Google and see what else is out there.

In the UK, you can check if your business name is already being used by looking at Companies House. Another option is to consider trademarking your business name. This is not a legal requirement, but it can provide valuable protection for your brand. A trademark is a type of intellectual property that helps distinguish your business and its products or services from others in the market.

Registering a trademark grants you exclusive rights to use the name in connection with the goods and services you offer, preventing others from using a similar name that could cause confusion among clients. However, trademark registration can be time-consuming and costly, so weigh the benefits against the potential drawbacks. Additionally, research existing trademarks to ensure your business name doesn't infringe on any existing registered trademarks.

Choosing a name for your practice can be a challenge that stops us from moving forward. Remember, nothing in your business is fixed in stone. If you are deliberating, remember, you can change it in the future. In fact, you may change it as your business evolves.

I spent far too much energy choosing a name in the first place. Then, I was very attached to it and upset when I had to change it. However, when I did change it, from CheshireCBT to Sarahdrees.co.uk, nothing happened at all. My clients barely noticed, and it made a lot more sense for my business. People choose a person as their therapist, so using your name provides that personal touch. On the other hand, Sophie chose the name Pocketsite.co.uk for her website, branding and resources business. Her long-term goal is to alter and expand her products and services, so a more generic name was preferable. I use the name 'Therapist Corner' for another section of my business. This broad term allows me to create many offerings or services within it.

Deciding whether to use your name for your business or create a different name depends on several factors. Here are some considerations to help you make the decision:

Choosing a Name

- If you're a solo professional, using your name can create a more personal connection with your clients and establish you as the expert in your field.
- For businesses where a team is involved or where you might want to expand your product or service offerings in the future, a more generic name could be more suitable. For example, if you want to have associates.

- If you want to build a strong personal brand and be recognised as an authority in your industry, using your name can be advantageous.
- Using your name can make separating your personal and professional lives more challenging, which could concern some individuals.
- Using your name may not always be the most memorable or unique choice, especially if you have a common name. Creating a distinctive business name can help you stand out from the competition and make it easier for clients to remember and find your business.

Finally, although you might not need a website for your business initially, most businesses do at some stage. When the time comes, you will want a domain name that matches your business name or at least reflects it. A domain name is an online address. Much like your home address is the location where you live, a domain name is where your website lives online. You can buy a domain name for about £10 a year. As soon as you have decided on the name of your business, I'd recommend purchasing the associated domain name so that it's yours for when you are ready to go online. Occasionally, people let a web designer or branding person buy their domain name. A few years down the line, when they want to move to another person to do their website, they realise they don't own their domain name and sometimes can't get ownership. Always purchase your own domain name or be sure you have the rights to transfer it into your name.

Name Considerations

- Keep it simple – your name should be easy to say and spell.
- Try to make it short, catchy and memorable.
- Consider the future. Choose a name that can grow with your business.
- Use your name for a more personal touch.
- Do a general search for your chosen name and see what comes up.
- Check for existing trademarks.
- Purchase the domain name.

The decision to use your name or another name for your business should be based on your specific circumstances, long-term goals and preferences. Also, the name you choose is not fixed in stone.

Your Marketplace Position

The second practical decision to consider when defining your business is the marketplace position for your private practice. Where does it sit in relation to other practices within a particular market? Essentially, it's about how you want your business to be perceived by your clients. It's the process of identifying and establishing your practice's image and identity in the minds of your clients, and it will shape how you financially plan and market your services.

It's helpful to consider this early on in the process of setting up because it will determine many aspects of the business, such as location, how much you invest in set-up costs and how you write about and describe your private practice. To determine your market position, consider your competition. You can analyse their market position and strategies to reach their ideal clients. Identify their strengths and weaknesses and use this information to differentiate your business from theirs.

Looking around the marketplace and your competitors can be tricky, especially in the early days as it's easy to spiral into comparison. Remember, someone might have a nice website, but it does not mean they have a thriving business behind the scenes. You do not know how their business is actually running.

Focus on looking at your competitor's business so you can do something different and bring your uniqueness to the world of private practice. Once researched, put your blinkers on and run your own race. Several other therapists might be doing something similar to you, but the good news is they are not you. You and your values are unique, and your uniqueness will be your business superpower.

When deciding your marketplace position, it's also important to consider your financial strategy. For example, when a business wants to offer a high-end service, it usually aims at more affluent clients and focuses on the quality and exclusivity of the product. On the other hand, when a business wants to offer a lower-price product, it targets a price-sensitive client base and focuses on affordability and value for money. This will be covered in greater depth in the following chapter.

It can be beneficial to establish a specific niche to focus on. This involves working with a specialised market segment, such as individuals with particular concerns or needs. For example, a therapist might specialise in working with perfectionism, chronic pain or OCD. By focusing on a specific niche, your private practice can cater directly to the needs of that group of clients and establish a reputation as a go-to resource for specialised support. This is a highly effective way to market your practice, as it helps you stand out from the crowd as you build your identity as an expert in your field.

Understanding your marketplace position supports you in developing effective marketing strategies and achieving financial success. You should continue to monitor your market position over time. By following these steps, you can ensure your business is positioned in the best way possible to reach and serve your ideal clients.

Conclusion

In this chapter, we've explored the first essential steps you need to take when setting up your private practice. You've learned that your journey can be both exhilarating and daunting. There are many things to consider and various steps to take.

The Done Diagram provides a roadmap to help you navigate the path ahead. It breaks down your journey into clear, practical steps, giving you an overview of what you need to do along the way. Make the decision to go into private practice and then define your ideas, build your strategy and set the objectives for your business and begin to organise them.

But remember, for us therapists, weaving strategy with planning isn't just ticking off a business checklist. It's about crafting a heartfelt roadmap for your practice, pinpointing where you stand today and painting a vivid picture of the haven you aspire to be for your clients. It embodies your purpose, your passion and the unique promise you extend to everyone seeking your guidance. This vision you're crafting? It's not merely about aesthetics or ambience, but the soul-soothing sanctuary you're committed to creating. As you pen down your business strategy, never lose sight of this: at the epicentre of every flourishing therapy practice lie values – deep-seated, unwavering principles. They serve as your compass, steering each choice, shaping every therapeutic session and guiding your strategic endeavours.

These core values? They are far more than mere words. They are the pillars upholding your practice, influencing the choices you make, the partnerships you forge, and resonating with those clients who will deeply connect with your ethos. Your values and vision truly set you apart, highlighting your unique brand of therapeutic magic.

We've already laid some foundational stones, from selecting a resonant name for your practice to getting a grip on your market position. Think of this chapter as your base camp. Expect more concrete action plans and specific, actionable steps to shape your practice as we progress. With each page, you are marching closer to your vision.

Business Plan Action

You have defined the name of your business and your position in the marketplace. You've also developed a business strategy that includes a clear mission for your practice, a vision for its future and the core values that will guide your business. Now it's time to write them out (see Figure 2.2) and have each element displayed prominently, keeping you focused and aligned as you develop your business.

BUSINESS PLANNING QUESTIONS

THE NAME OF YOUR BUSINESS

YOUR MARKETPLACE POSITION

WRITE OUT YOUR MISSION STATEMENT

WRITE OUT YOUR VISION

WRITE OUT THE VALUES OF YOUR THERAPY PRACTICE

Figure 2.2 Business plan actions: Write out the name of your business, marketplace position, mission, vision and values.

Chapter 3

Money Matters

Introduction

Effective money management is crucial for building a successful and sustainable private practice. Did you know poor financial management is one of the most common reasons small businesses fail in their first year?

Running a financially sustainable business is beneficial for both you and your clients. It ensures your business can support you in having a good work-life balance, adequate support, supervision, training and time off without economic anxieties. In turn, financial stability allows you to provide the best possible service for your clients.

This chapter will explore how you can confidently build a financially viable private practice that aligns with your objectives and values. I will guide you through identifying and overcoming some of the mindset obstacles, mastering the art of setting appropriate fees and understanding your operational costs.

Additionally, we will discuss establishing financial goals, building a financial buffer, periodically reviewing your financial performance and maintaining the profitability of your business. By creating good money management habits from the start, you will avoid the common financial pitfalls and stresses associated with building a business, leaving you free to focus your energy on what you love most – providing high-quality, effective therapy.

Start with Financial Advice

Disclaimer: I'm not an accountant and do not have any financial training. The advice in this chapter is based on my personal experience of running a private practice for over ten years.

I'd recommend you get some independent financial advice and consider working with an accountant. Meet with a few accountants to get a comprehensive overview of your options. It will be a long-term collaboration, so take time selecting the right person for you and your business. Meeting a few allows you to gather all the necessary information and choose the best accountant to work with.

I was a few years into running my business when I did this. I wish I'd done it from the very start. Although it adds to your expenses, getting expert guidance to

DOI: 10.4324/9781003401391-4

support you in navigating the complex financial aspects of running a business is invaluable. Ultimately, it will save you money and time.

Financial Structure

Your accountant can advise you on the financial structure of your business. You have two options in the UK: setting up as a sole trader, or a limited company. This varies depending on where you live and the country's laws and regulations.

A sole trader is the simplest business structure, where one individual owns and runs the entire business. A sole trader can keep all profits after deducted taxes but is liable for all their business losses. When you're a sole trader, you are your business. It's straightforward to set yourself up as self-employed, and start-up costs are low. You keep all the profits and benefit from maximum privacy. Adjusting the structure or closing your business is relatively easy if circumstances change.

Advantages of a Sole Trader

- You get 100% profit.
- Easy to set up and get started.
- Reduced administration.
- Fewer accountancy costs.

Disadvantages of a Sole Trader

- You have unlimited liability.
- You are fully responsible for your business.
- It can be less tax efficient than Ltd.
- They are not seen as being as professional as a Ltd company.

In contrast, setting up a limited company means your private practice will be an entity in its own right and you will be the director. As its owner, you are legally responsible for its debts only to the extent of your invested money. Running your private practice as a limited company provides the potential for more profitability, as they tend to be more tax efficient. They qualify for a broader range of allowances and tax-deductible expenses and can generate more investment and lending opportunities.

Limited company status also offers some liability protection. Simply put, your personal assets, like your house, will be secure if your company runs into trouble. This is because a limited company is seen as a separate legal entity, a legal 'person' in its own right. In many ways, being a limited company director has greater professional status than being a sole trader; when people see 'Ltd' after the name of your business, this can increase credibility and trust.

However, there are some downsides too. You'll encounter more financial administration, which takes time to understand, and face more rigid taxation rules. Directors of limited companies have certain legal obligations, and you'll also have less privacy than a sole trader.

Advantages of a Limited Company

- You can be more tax efficient.
- Losses and debts aren't yours personally.
- Limited companies can be perceived as more professional and established.
- Some businesses will only work with limited companies, so it's a consideration if you want to provide corporate workshops.
- You can't be personally sued.

Disadvantages of a Limited Company

- Your business has to prepare annual accounts.
- There is more financial administration and therefore, costs involved.
- There is less privacy as your annual financial accounts are open to the public.
- Taxation rules are more rigid.

I ran my private practice as a sole trader for the first eight years of business. Then, at one of my annual business reviews, my accountant advised that moving to a limited company would be more tax efficient. I had also started doing more corporate workshops, so a limited company was more closely aligned with my business's direction.

Choosing to be a sole trader or a limited company is an individual decision based on where you are and how you want your business to look going forward. In either scenario, I'd advise working with an accountant you can trust so they can provide expert advice and guide you in the right direction.

Business Banking

Do you need a business bank account? In short, yes! All the revenue for your business should be paid into a separate bank account. You will need to account for all expenses going out and payments coming into your business. Make sure to keep all your receipts and raise an invoice for client sessions. I have one business account and then within it, I have different pots for profit, expenses, tax and one for my wage; I find it easy to separate money in this way. It keeps me organised and ensures I don't think all the money in my bank is mine!

Reasons for a Separate Bank Account

- A separate bank account makes it easier to manage your business finances. You can track income and expenses more efficiently and accurately. It makes tax reporting and accounting simpler and more efficient.
- In many countries, it is a legal requirement for businesses to have a separate bank account to keep business transactions separate from personal finances.
- Having a business bank account shows that you are running your business professionally.
- A separate business bank account can help protect your personal assets from legal or financial issues arising while running your business.

Setting up a separate business bank account can provide legal protection and transparency and simplify your financial management. Some accountants will recommend bank accounts that will link up to their accounting systems, which can be useful and highlights the benefits of speaking with an accountant from the start.

Insurance

In his book *The Meaningful Money Handbook* (2018), Pete Matthew talks about the three fundamental principles for financial success. First, spend less than you earn. Second, insure against disaster, and third, invest wisely. We can have all our financial goals in place, but if disaster strikes, it means nothing. Insuring against disaster provides a financial foundation in case the worst happens. The problem with insurance is that it can feel like we are paying for nothing until we need it. Setting up insurance from the start is a good habit to be in. Again, I'd encourage you to discuss your options with a financial advisor. The primary insurances I have taken out are life insurance, critical illness and income protection.

Pensions

Being self-employed also requires us to take responsibility for our own retirement planning. Several pension options are available, and it's essential to understand them to make informed decisions about your retirement savings. Here are some standard pension options for self-employed individuals in the UK:

- *Personal pension:* A personal pension is a defined contribution pension that you can set up directly with a pension provider. You choose the provider and make regular or one-off contributions to your pension pot. The pension provider will claim tax relief on your behalf and add it to your pot. The funds are invested, and the growth is tax-free. You can access your pension pot upon reaching the minimum pension age (currently 55).
- *Stakeholder pension:* A stakeholder pension is a type of personal pension with specific features, such as capped charges and low minimum contribution limits, making it more accessible for those with lower incomes or irregular earnings. Stakeholder pensions also offer a default investment option for those who don't want to make investment decisions.
- *Self-invested personal pension (SIPP):* A SIPP is a type of personal pension that offers more flexibility in investment choices. With a SIPP, you have greater control over the investments within your pension pot, allowing you to select from a wider range of assets. However, this option may involve higher fees and is generally more suitable for experienced investors.

The UK also has the National Employment Savings Trust (NEST). NEST is a government-backed pension scheme originally designed for the auto-enrolment of employees but is also available to self-employed individuals. It operates similarly to a personal pension, with contributions invested in a pension pot that grows over time.

Pension options, rules and regulations change over time, so it is essential to consult with a financial advisor or research the most up-to-date information when planning your retirement savings strategy.

Money Mindset

Money is not just a tangible resource; it's also a mindset. Our beliefs, attitudes and behaviours towards money inform our 'money mindset.' They are shaped and developed from our past and present experiences. For example, someone who has grown up in a family struggling with finances may develop a scarcity mindset, which can cause them to feel anxious about money, not want to invest in their business, worry about financial security and always feel like they need to save or be avoidant of facing their finances.

In contrast, individuals who have enjoyed financial security and success may develop a more confident and abundance-oriented mindset. They may feel comfortable investing in their business, putting together a financial plan, regularly reviewing their goals confidently and not feeling the need to focus too much on money.

I used to avoid looking at my finances. It was a daunting task I didn't want to engage with, so I convinced myself it wasn't necessary since my business was still in its early stages. As time passed and problems arose, I realised the impact of my avoidance. By neglecting my finances, I had undercharged and overspent for a while. I didn't have a financial buffer and had missed crucial opportunities to make informed decisions about my business's growth and profitability. My finances always sat just on the edge of an overdraft, proving my money mindset was right: there's just 'never enough.' I would find myself accepting referrals from companies even if my values didn't align with theirs, making me unhappy in my work.

For a while, I didn't understand the concept of cash flow. Cash flow is the movement of money in and out of your business account over a specific period of time. A healthy cash flow means you have enough money to cover all your outgoings. Not understanding the importance of this meant I was busy working with clients but not getting paid for 90 days after I'd finished treatment with them. This situation was financially dire and very stressful. I learned the hard way that if I wanted to work with a referral company on these terms, I could see only a couple of their clients, and I needed to prioritise self-funding clients who paid on the day of their session, thus balancing out cash flow.

> Face your finances head-on and make it a priority to stay on top of them.

What's Your Money Mindset?

We all have a money story which has shaped our beliefs around money. As Morgan Housel insightfully put it in 2020, 'Money is a story we tell ourselves and we're all bad storytellers.' Recognising this can be powerful in understanding our financial behaviours. To help you better understand your money mindset, I've created an exercise that will guide you through a series of questions and prompts. These are designed to uncover your beliefs, values and attitudes around money that may be holding you back from writing a more accurate and constructive financial narrative for yourself.

Discovering Your Money Mindset

- Take a few deep breaths to calm your mind and relax your body. Allow yourself to be fully present in the moment.
- Ask yourself at least five times, 'Money is?' Then write out your answers.
- Think about your relationship with money. What are your thoughts and feelings when you think about money? Do you feel abundant, or do you feel like there is never enough?
- Identify any limiting beliefs you may have around money. These could include thoughts such as 'I'll never be able to make enough money' or 'Money doesn't grow on trees.' Write them down.
- Next, spend time reframing these limiting beliefs in a way that will be more useful for you as a business owner. For example, if you wrote, 'Money doesn't grow on trees,' you could reframe it as 'While money may not grow on trees, there are many ways to create wealth and abundance in my life.'
- Ask yourself – What are your top financial priorities?
- How do you feel about spending money on yourself? How do you feel about spending money on others?
- How do all these beliefs affect your actions and decisions?
- Think about your relationship with money. Do you want to feel more abundant and financially secure?
- How will financial security impact you, your business and the service you can provide for your clients?
- Write down your goals for your money mindset.

This exercise will help you identify whether you have an abundant or lack mindset around money. It will also help you understand some underlying beliefs, attitudes and thoughts that may influence your relationship with money. I believe this is essential knowledge for all new business owners; Jen Sincero (2017) states that 'Our thoughts become our reality. When it comes to money, if you focus on lack and scarcity, that's what you'll attract.' With more awareness of our money mindset, we have more choices over how we move forward with our finances and start developing a more positive and abundant relationship with money.

It's OK to Make Money

Therapists are notorious for undervaluing their services. It's difficult for others to value our work when we don't value it ourselves. It concerns me when I hear from people undercharging for a few reasons. Firstly, I know the dedication, time and years of training it takes to deliver and maintain delivery of effective therapy. Secondly, I feel passionately that we should value care for others at every stage of life. Historically, caring professions have always been dominated by women, we know that as a society, we are still trying to bridge the gender pay gap and resolve the financial inequalities faced by women, so there's still a lot of baggage attached to how people are paid in the caring professions.

To some extent, the traditional undervaluing of work in the caring professions is linked to the historical perception of women's roles and their worth in the work-force. As we strive for pay equity, we must continue challenging these outdated notions and ensure fair compensation for all professionals in the caring fields. With this in mind, as you go forward in your private practice, you are paving the way for how therapy is valued.

Another useful mindset shift is to remove yourself from the equation and start seeing the therapy you deliver as a service your business provides. It's not you personally that has decided your hourly fee. It's the business you run which determines the price you charge. The financial facts of your business set your hourly rate based on what it requires to be sustainable. Instead of saying, 'I charge £ . . . an hour,' begin by saying, 'The cost of a therapy session is £ . . .'

Therapists play a crucial role in helping individuals overcome mental health challenges and lead fulfilling lives. We invest significant time, energy and money into obtaining the education and training necessary to provide high-quality care to our clients. Reflecting on the words of Suze Orman from 1997, 'Value is not determined by those who set the price but by those who choose to pay it,' we see that the true worth of our services extends beyond monetary compensation. The value of therapy is multifaceted, encompassing the profound, positive changes in the lives of those we help – the emotional resilience, improved relationships and personal growth. As with any profession, therapists need to be fairly compensated for their skills and expertise. Such compensation should acknowledge not only the tangible efforts we make but also the intangible, life-enhancing benefits that our clients receive. In essence, our fees should mirror the comprehensive value we provide, ensuring that we honour the depth and breadth of our contribution to our clients' well-being.

In private practice, we offer people another way to protect and improve their mental health. The practice you create is just one piece of a larger puzzle. There are many options out there for people to choose from. The more choices people have, the better. When I get an enquiry from someone who needs support but can't afford to work with me, which has happened no matter what I charge, I will spend time with them to find and access support from other sources. Therapists who work from home can have lower expenses and, therefore, a lower hourly rate. Several charities offer means-tested therapy, or in the UK, there's the National Health Service. It's worth having a few alternative options for clients if what you charge is not within their budget. When your business is financially stable, you have more flexibility to go that extra mile for people, which is rewarding, especially when running a values-based business.

By earning a good income, therapists can better support themselves and their families, invest in ongoing education and professional development, and maintain a healthy work-life balance. Additionally, fair compensation enables therapists to continue providing quality care to their clients without being burdened by financial stress, allowing them to focus on their client's needs and achieve positive outcomes.

Consider how you would deliver therapy if you had a good work-life balance and money wasn't a concern. How much supervision would you have? What training would you do? How much time would you spend on reflection? Then, consider the impact this would have on your clients. How differently would you be able to show up for them? Ultimately, making good money as a therapist is not only acceptable but necessary to ensure you can continue providing valuable services to your clients and contribute to the mental health field as a whole.

Setting Your Financial Goals

Responsible financial management is essential when running a value-based private practice because a value-based business prioritises its social and environmental impact alongside its financial profitability. It involves creating financial plans and goals that align with the values of the private practice.

Reflect on how you may want to make a social, community or environmental impact. You might invest in sustainable materials, aim to employ people from the local community, have fair labour practices, or get involved in carbon offset programs.

I've been able to support a charity by assigning 10% of profits made from a digital product I sell to support a cause that's important to me.

I prioritise working with female-led businesses and using local services to maintain and support my office; who I work with is always a considered investment in terms of its impact.

Profit First Goal

Reading *Profit First* by Mike Michalowicz (2017) transformed my business's finances a few years ago. I'd highly recommend adding it to your reading list.

The book's premise is that having a goal of saving your profit first ensures you always have a healthy profit in your business. This principle aligns with James Clear's observation 'You don't rise to the level of your goals; you fall to the level of your systems.' Clear (2018) statement is a reminder that the sustainability of our financial success hinges not just on our goals but on the robustness of the systems we put in place. By setting aside a portion of our revenue as profit from the outset, we ensure that our private practice doesn't just survive but thrives. When we prioritise profit as a goal and set aside a portion of revenue to cover it right from the start, we are ensuring our private practice generates real, sustainable value. This means we can make a bigger impact around us. It's a great habit to get into. Establishing reliable and effective financial systems, goals and habits will prove to be invaluable, creating a roadmap for success that helps you stay focused and motivated.

Five Key Financial Goals to Set

Step 1 – Decide on Your Business Profit

Profit is the amount of money a business earns after deducting all its expenses, wages, taxes and other costs from its revenue, which is the money the business makes. The profit in a business builds financial stability, enabling it to pay off debts and build reserves to weather unexpected economic downturns or other challenges. In the first few years of private practice, saving your profit can be difficult, but it's an important habit to begin from the very start. Even if it's just a few per cent of your monthly revenue, it will provide you with crucial financial security and peace of mind. Ultimately, starting with profit first can help you create a thriving, financially secure business that supports your goals, values and aspirations.

Step 2 – Know Your Expenses

A business expense is any cost that is necessary to operate a business and generate revenue. Make sure to track and manage expenses, keep accurate records of your expenses to comply with tax regulations and take advantage of tax deductions. Business expenses are tax deductible, so keep all the receipts for anything you buy for your business. Estimating some of your costs at the beginning may be necessary – for example, taxes. I recommend setting aside 25% of your income in the first year. This will buffer any unexpected costs and help you avoid financial stress. Consider what you will need for therapy room costs, your wage, pension, insurance, equipment, marketing costs, supervision, training, travel and other overheads. I keep a list of my regular expenses on a spreadsheet and review it monthly, adding in any other expenses that arise throughout the month.

Step 3 – What Will You Pay Yourself?

Go through all your personal expenses and outgoings, including personal savings, to determine what you need to live on comfortably each month. You can then easily scale this up to establish what you need for the year.

Step 4 – Business Investments

Consider how much money you need to invest in your business each year so it continues to run efficiently and expands (if that's what you hope to do).

Investments might include new equipment such as computers, software, office decoration and maintenance or websites, marketing, supervision and annual training requirements.

Step 5 — Decide on Your Revenue Goal

Revenue is the total amount of money your private practice will bring in each year from the work you do before deducting expenses, taxes, investments and other costs. So, do your sums and determine what you need to pay yourself each year. Then, estimate what it will cost to run your private practice each year. Add these two amounts together, and this is the revenue you need. You might want a goal that is above this, and you might aim to increase it each year. By setting a revenue goal, you can focus your efforts on the activities that drive growth and track your progress over time.

With your goals in place, the financial structure begins to take shape. From this, you can work out the percentages of how your revenue will be distributed, helping you stay on track financially because you have clarity around what you need to achieve.

Creating a Financial Plan

When you are starting out in private practice, the absence of a regular salary can leave you feeling vulnerable, anxious, insecure, and desperate to attract paying clients. Financial goal setting and planning is the antidote.

Creating a plan is about building the structure you need to meet your financial goals. Start by clearly defining your short-term, medium-term and long-term financial goals. Determine when you want to accomplish each goal, and then create a timeline that outlines the steps you need to take to get there. Deciding what your income will be made up of is a key part of this. There are many ways to create income in private practice and having a few income streams is sensible. Head to the end of the chapter for a financial plan template you can use.

Financial planning is an ongoing process. You will need to regularly review and update your plan to ensure it aligns with your business values, goals and needs. This will help you stay on track and adjust your business as needed.

Setting Your Hourly Rate

With your financial foundations in place, you can now work out your hourly rate. As soon as I spent time developing the correct hourly rate for my business, based on careful consideration of all the facts, I felt much more confident asking for payment. I finally understood why it is what it is. What you charge should be based on the facts of what it costs for your private practice to operate rather than feelings about what you 'should' be charging or your perception of what others can afford.

As discussed in Chapter 2, being clear on your marketplace position is important when creating a financial plan for your practice. To attract more affluent clients, you will charge a premium for your services. However, this may also require investing more in your business. Alternatively, attracting less wealthy clients will require you to price your services lower, and therefore, you need to focus on keeping your business costs to a minimum to maintain profitability. Knowing the general economic position of the clients you hope to work with ensures you can

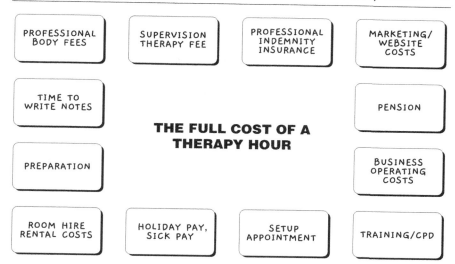

Image 3.1 Full cost of a therapy hour

develop a financial plan tailored to their needs and your business's goals. The next step is to consider how many clients you can comfortably see in a week. Once you have this number, add two more, allowing for cancellations or missed appointments. A common mistake I see therapists make is that they can overestimate how many clients they can see weekly. Remember to account for the time you need to run your business, along with the time required for preparation, and reflection and note-writing following sessions.

Image 3.1 shows some of the elements you need to consider when pricing an hour of therapy.

Therapist Fee Calculator

Designed by Sophie A. Wood, founder of Pocketsite.co.uk, this valuable tool was created to assist therapists in determining their optimal hourly rate. The innovative calculator focuses on your specific financial requirements to ensure your practice thrives and continues to support clients effectively. It takes into account all your business overheads and their impact on your fee. The fee calculator takes the guesswork out of pricing, providing a more informed and sustainable approach to charging for your services.

A useful exercise to do at some point is to spend a week recording all the hours you spend on your business seeing clients and outside of this, too. Then, divide the number of hours worked by the income you made for that week and divide the hours you worked by this to provide you with your hourly rate for that week. I guarantee you will be surprised! You can also work out your hourly fee by using the tool shown in Image 3.2.

SET YOUR HOURLY RATE - THE THERAPIST FEE CALCULATOR

THERE IS A DIGITAL VERSION OF THIS ON POCKETSITE.CO.UK

ADD YOUR BUSINESS OVERHEADS INCLUDING SALARY

- MY SALARY, WHAT DO YOU WANT YOUR ANNUAL SALARY TO BE:

- ADD 30% - TO COVER TAXES:

- ADD BUSINESS EXPENSES PER YEAR:

- ADD IN A PROFIT MARGIN, USUALLY 10%:

- ADD THESE AMOUNTS TOGETHER:

THIS IS THE AMOUNT YOU NEED TO EARN IN A YEAR

Image 3.2 Therapist fee calculator x 2

When you work out your hourly rate based on facts, you will feel much more confident, but it can still feel a little scary at the start. This is completely normal.

There can be a huge temptation to charge the same as other local therapists or keep your rates as low as possible based on the idea that lower rates mean more referrals. It doesn't, and even if it did, your practice wouldn't be financially sustainable. All businesses spend a lot of time and energy getting the pricing just right. Whatever your rate is, there will always be clients who think you are overcharging. Like we all do when shopping for products and services, they just need to find the right fit for them and their budget. Your priority needs to be building a financially stable practice so you can stay operating for longer and make a bigger impact.

Charging Transparency

Will you be transparent about your hourly rate? Some therapists choose not to share their hourly rates, while others, like me, have them clearly displayed on their websites. There are a few reasons therapists keep their rates private. They may

- HOW MANY WEEKS WILL YOU WORK IN A YEAR:

  [   ]

- HOW MANY HOURS OF THERAPY WILL YOU ON AVERAGE DO IN A WEEK?

  [   ]

- X TIMES THE AMOUNT OF HOURS YOU WILL WORK IN A WEEK BY THE NUMBER OF WEEKS YOU WILL WORK IN A YEAR – THIS GIVES YOU THE NUMBER OF HOURS OF THERAPY YOU WILL DO IN A YEAR

  [   ]

- THEN DIVIDE THE AMOUNT YOU NEED TO EARN IN TOTAL BY THE NUMBER OF HOURS OF THERAPY YOU WILL DELIVER

  [   ]

- THIS SHOWS YOU WHAT YOU NEED TO CHARGE PER HOUR

  [   ]

Image 3.2 (Continued)

have a sliding scale of rates due to working with clients across economic markets. Although this is a viable option, it can be complicated to operationalise. They may feel potential clients will reach out to ask about rates, allowing them to discuss their needs and see if they're the right fit.

If you were looking for a therapist, what would you prefer? Put yourself in your client's place and consider which option fits with your values. For me, if someone doesn't have their prices clearly displayed, I would not pursue it any further because clarity and transparency are important values for me when I'm choosing to work with someone.

An exception might be if you offer concessions. I worked in the NHS for many years, so I offer a discount for clients who work there, and I discuss this with them at their first session. I don't advertise this because I don't want other demographics to feel like they are overpaying. It's a personal decision for me. You might decide to offer something similar for students or another demographic.

When to Take Payment

Many therapists adopt the practice of receiving payment 24 hours in advance or at the time of booking a session. This can be seamlessly managed, particularly if your website has an integrated booking and payment system. My preference, however, is to accept payment at the end of each session, whether it's conducted online or face-to-face. Reflect on the rationale behind your choice. What's the core reason? Is it a concern about not being paid, or worries about client commitment? Ask yourself, should these concerns be the foundation of your practice, or would you rather build it on principles of trust, respect and transparency? Consider your fundamental values. Once again, step into your client's shoes and think about what approach feels more approachable and fairer from their perspective.

Block Bookings

Block booking clients for therapy sessions can have both pros and cons. On the positive side, it can help ensure clients have regular access to therapy, which can be particularly beneficial for those with ongoing or chronic mental health issues. It can also help to streamline scheduling and reduce the administrative workload associated with booking individual appointments.

However, there are also potential downsides to block bookings. For example, clients may feel pressured to commit to a certain number of sessions upfront, which might be overwhelming. It can also create a sense of rigidity in the therapeutic relationship, which may not be conducive to the process. Additionally, it can get complicated if a client needs to cancel or reschedule a session, and a client may decide they don't require all the sessions they have booked, which may increase administration.

Furthermore, block bookings can impact financial planning for both the therapist and the client. While it may offer a predictable income stream for the therapist, it could pose a significant upfront cost for the client. This might exclude those who cannot afford to pay for multiple sessions in advance. Also, therapists might find it challenging to accommodate new clients if their schedules are heavily booked in advance.

It's essential to weigh these pros and cons and consider your approach to block booking in alignment with your values and the needs of your clientele. Offering flexibility, such as the option to book a few sessions at a time or providing a mix of block and individual session bookings, could be a balanced solution. Ultimately, the decision should prioritise the well-being and comfort of your clients while ensuring your practice remains manageable and effective.

Payment Methods

There are several ways of taking payment for your services and it's beneficial to have a few options. In the last few years, I've used a card machine, which is the most popular option for face-to-face sessions. I can also provide a digital payment link for online sessions. Very few people choose to pay with cash, and cheques are currently being phased out. Another option is to use a payment processing service such as PayPal, which allows clients to pay online and by credit or debit card. Some therapists also use electronic billing systems that automatically bill clients and process payments.

You can provide your bank details and allow people to make a bank transfer. I do provide this option for online sessions. Whichever method you choose, it is important to consider the fees associated with each payment method, as well as any security measures that may be necessary to protect client information. You should always research a payment provider's data protection policies. Ultimately, the payment method chosen will depend on your preferences and the needs of your clients.

Non-Payments

As private practitioners, we often work with individuals during challenging times in their lives. This can impact their ability to show up at their best and may result in missed appointments, non-payments, or delayed payments. This needs to be accounted for in our financial planning so that when it happens, it doesn't throw us into a financial panic. Instead, we should be able to respond to it as part of the client's treatment plan in a boundaried and contained way.

This is the exception rather than the rule. Ninety-nine per cent of people will be respectful and pay for the services they use. However, when they don't, it can be an unexpected shock. It can also be upsetting, especially the first few times it happens. I see some therapists who decide to run their practice from the perspective of the 1% who don't respect their service, imposing harsh rules and boundaries from a place of mistrust and fear. I can completely understand why, and I've certainly been tempted to put such measures in place on occasion. However, suppose we return to the client's experience again when they land on your website and read through the conditions and boundaries of your practice. In that case, the most honest and respectful might be put off and offended by the regulations.

The key is to expect it to happen, so you are not as surprised and allow for it within your financial planning, therapy agreements and contract terms. You should also establish a protocol for managing late payments and non-payments. This way, when it occurs, you have a system in place you can follow.

There are several options to support you in claiming back payments that have not been paid. During my private practice years, I've only had to chase payment a few times.

I issue an invoice after the session, then again at the end of that month as a polite reminder. If I get no response, I would then send a pre-action letter. Usually, this prompts payment, but if not, going through the small claims court is an inexpensive, straightforward process. In the UK, the government website lays out clear instructions.

Late Cancellations

If you start from the position of trusting your client and being respectful of what is happening for them, late cancellations will be a straightforward process.

Again, make sure you have a policy in place. Within my pricing, I've accounted for the likelihood that everyone might miss at least one appointment. This allows me to use that first missed appointment or late cancellation as an opportunity to remind the person of my policies. If I ever need to cancel an appointment at short notice, it also allows some grace for me too. Your policy does need to work both ways. If you have charged a client for a late cancellation and then something crops up for you at short notice, how will you compensate for your client's time?

The policy I have in place is that I ask for 24 hours' notice to cancel an appointment. If a client gives less than 24 hours, I charge half the cost of a session to cover my incurred costs, but generally, even with one hour's notice, it means I can catch up on administration. If I don't receive any notice, I charge for the entire hour because I will have waited for them to arrive.

As I said before, on the first occasion, it's an opportunity to remind people of my policy. If a client is going to be unreliable and may not fully engage in attending sessions, you begin to recognise it over time and be more precise about your boundaries. The attendance rate in private practice is higher than anywhere I've ever worked. In previous roles, I was able to rely on cancellations to keep up to date with my administration, but not anymore.

The first couple of times you experience a late cancellation or no-show, it's really frustrating, so do talk it through with your support or supervisor. Work through the frustrations, recognising these are your own feelings, so you don't let them enter your dialogue with the client.

You can also reframe the situation and see it as an opportunity to review and improve your policies and processes. Putting harsh or overly strict rules in place after a bad experience can be tempting, but you shouldn't let one person shape your business. Remember your core values and act accordingly. With experience, no-shows will have very little impact on your business.

Changing Your Hourly Rate

Set a date in your calendar to have an annual financial review where you go through all your figures and take into account the current rate of inflation. This is the rate at which the general level of prices for goods and services in an economy increases over a period of time. It results in a decrease in the purchasing power of money, meaning that each unit of currency buys fewer goods and services than it did before. Inflation is typically measured by a price index, such as the Consumer Price Index (CPI) or the Producer Price Index (PPI), which tracks the changes in prices of a representative basket of goods and services over time.

I have worked with some clients for a long time and when I increase my prices, this is for new clients that are coming to see me. Longer-term clients that are 'grandfathered' on the older rate will benefit from working with me on a reduced rate. I do still review this annually but increase their rates at a slower pace.

For self-employed individuals, it's crucial to consider the impact of inflation on your income and adjust your rates or fees accordingly. Over time, inflation erodes the purchasing power of money, making goods and services more expensive. If you don't adjust your income to keep up with inflation, you may find that your actual income (the income adjusted for inflation) decreases, leading to a decline in your overall standard of living. When you set out your therapy agreements, it's good practice to say that you do an annual financial review so that clients know your rates may alter.

Conclusion

Running a private therapy practice involves both delivering therapy sessions and managing a business. Good financial management is key to ensuring your practice thrives and is sustainable. As Jen Sincero (2017) suggests, changing your beliefs and habits around money is essential. Creating a financial plan and cultivating good money management habits can help avoid common financial pitfalls, allowing you to focus on providing high-quality therapy.

Here are some condensed key points from this chapter:

- *Seek financial advice:* Consulting an accountant can help you establish your business's financial structure.
- *Set a separate business account:* This aids in easier management and offers legal protection.
- *Plan for retirement:* Consulting a financial advisor is crucial for pension planning.
- *Set a confident hourly rate:* Base your rate on financial facts rather than subjective factors or mindset.
- *Work on money mindset:* Understand your beliefs around money to foster a positive financial relationship.

Therapists often undervalue their services due to historical perceptions. By valuing your work fairly, you contribute to changing how therapy is perceived and compensated. Financial stability in your business allows for flexibility and the opportunity to offer value-based services. Here are five key financial goals you need to have in place:

- Decide on your business profit.
- Know your business expenses.
- Determine your salary.
- Understand business investments.
- Set a revenue goal.

Remember to set your hourly rate based on operational costs and the additional time required for therapy preparation and business management. Avoid comparing your rates to others, and be prepared for client-related financial challenges by having a protocol for managing late or non-payments.

Lastly, consider the impact of inflation on your income and adjust rates accordingly. Financial planning is an ongoing process, and adapting to changes is part of running a sustainable, profitable business. As Mary Kay Ash wisely said, 'Don't limit yourself. Many people limit themselves to what they think they can do. You can go as far as your mind lets you. What you believe, remember, you can achieve.' Embrace this mindset to push beyond limitations and achieve the financial success and sustainability your practice deserves.

Business Plan Actions – Financial Plan Template

Following the steps shown in Figures 3.3–3.5, fill out what will be the financial plan for your therapy business.

FINANCIAL PLANNING TEMPLATE

SETTING SMART FINANCIAL GOALS

SPECIFIC: YOUR GOAL SHOULD BE WELL-DEFINED AND CLEAR.
MEASURABLE: IDENTIFY SPECIFIC METRICS OR INDICATORS THAT WILL
HELP YOU MEASURE YOUR PROGRESS.

ACHIEVABLE: YOUR GOAL SHOULD BE REALISTIC AND ATTAINABLE.
CONSIDER YOUR RESOURCES, SKILLS AND TIME FRAME WHEN SETTING
YOUR GOAL. IT SHOULD BE CHALLENGING BUT NOT SO DIFFICULT THAT
IT'S IMPOSSIBLE TO ACHIEVE.

RELEVANT: YOUR GOAL SHOULD BE RELEVANT TO YOUR OBJECTIVES AND
ASPIRATIONS. IT SHOULD ALIGN WITH YOUR VALUES, MISSION AND LONG-
TERM VISION.

TIME-BOUND: YOUR GOALS SHOULD HAVE A CLEAR DEADLINE OR TIME
FRAME. THIS HELPS YOU STAY FOCUSED AND MOTIVATED AND ENSURES
THAT YOU'RE MAKING PROGRESS TOWARDS YOUR GOAL IN A TIMELY
MANNER.

WRITE OUT YOUR FINANCIAL GOALS MAKING SURE THEY ARE SMART

-
-
-
-
-

Figure 3.3 Financial planning 1: Write out your SMART goals.

FINANCIAL PLAN

SET A DATE FOR YOUR ANNUAL FINANCIAL REVIEW:

LIST OUT ALL THE WAYS YOU GENERATE YOUR INCOME, E.G., CLIENT WORK, SUPERVISION, TRAINING, ETC

-
-
-
-
-

Figure 3.4 Financial planning 2: List out the ways you will make an income.

FINANCIAL PLAN

AN ANNUAL FINANCIAL PLAN FOR A SMALL BUSINESS TYPICALLY INCLUDES SEVERAL KEY COMPONENTS.

- REVENUE FORECAST: A REVENUE FORECAST PREDICTS THE AMOUNT OF MONEY YOUR BUSINESS WILL BRING IN OVER THE NEXT YEAR. THIS CAN BE BROKEN DOWN BY PRODUCT OR SERVICE.

- EXPENSE BUDGET: AN EXPENSE BUDGET OUTLINES ALL THE COSTS ASSOCIATED WITH RUNNING YOUR BUSINESS, INCLUDING RENT, UTILITIES, SUPERVISION, TRAINING, MARKETING AND SUPPLIES. BE SURE TO INCLUDE BOTH FIXED COSTS (SUCH AS RENT) AND VARIABLE COSTS (SUCH AS MARKETING EXPENSES THAT MAY VARY MONTHLY).

- CASH FLOW PROJECTION: A CASH FLOW PROJECTION SHOWS HOW MUCH CASH YOUR BUSINESS WILL HAVE ON HAND AT ANY GIVEN TIME OVER THE NEXT YEAR. THIS IS IMPORTANT TO ENSURE THAT YOU HAVE ENOUGH CASH TO COVER YOUR EXPENSES AND TAKE ADVANTAGE OF POSSIBLE OPPORTUNITIES.

BY INCLUDING THESE COMPONENTS IN YOUR ANNUAL FINANCIAL PLAN, YOU CAN ENSURE THAT YOU HAVE A COMPREHENSIVE UNDERSTANDING OF YOUR BUSINESS'S FINANCIAL HEALTH AND ARE WELL-EQUIPPED TO MAKE INFORMED DECISIONS ABOUT ITS FUTURE.

Figure 3.5 Financial planning 3: Write out your forecast, budget and cash flow predictions.

Chapter 4

Building a Caseload

In the first year of running a private practice, the number one worry that often keeps us up at night is whether we'll have enough referrals to make ends meet.

It was certainly one of mine. In fact, it was such a driving force that I registered with every available referral option. Until I found myself working with several companies that did not align with my values. However, they were like a safety blanket because I wasn't sure I could build a caseload of my own accord; this mindset kept me stuck for a while.

Client referrals are the lifeblood of your private practice, forming the backbone of your income. This chapter will explore various referral generation options to help you build a robust caseload. Our goal is to provide you with a comprehensive overview, allowing you to select the best strategies that resonate with your business values, ultimately shaping a sustainable and resilient caseload.

When I was working for numerous insurance companies and referral agencies, it felt like I had gone from having one boss to having ten, each with different protocols and systems to use. Ultimately, I was not enjoying my business. I call this strategy the 'Scattergun Method' (it didn't work for me). I had a rethink, became more strategic, considered the ideal clients I wanted to work with and established a long-term goal to work with mostly self-referring clients. Why? I find it very rewarding to work with people who have done their research, know about my approach and want to work with me. I narrowed down the third parties I was registered with until I only took referrals from companies more aligned with how I wanted to work. One of the benefits of working in private practice is that you can choose who you work with, aligning your specialist interest, expertise and skills with the right clients who will benefit the most from working with you.

Who Do You Want to Work With?

When I decided to move from the scattergun approach to being more strategic, this is the question I started with. I returned to the Done Diagram model (see Chapter 2) and decided who I wanted to work with and which clients would benefit most from my work. You may want to work with referral companies, especially when you are starting out, as it takes time to build your practice up. However,

DOI: 10.4324/9781003401391-5

reflecting on the clients you would like on your caseload is still useful, so you can eventually work towards this. It can also help you say no to referrals that might not be a good fit.

Ask Yourself

- Who are the clients you have most connected with?
- Who are the clients that enjoy working with you?
- Who are the clients who do well in therapy with you?
- What types of clients or presentations do you want to work with?
- Where does your expertise lie?

As you go through these questions, you should start to notice a theme. These are the clients you most want to work with and who, in turn, will want to work with you too, creating a rewarding and enriching caseload.

Who Do You NOT Want to Work With?

This is another important question to consider. The truth is, we can't be a perfect fit for everyone. We don't have the skills, experience and expertise to support every client. Some client groups have higher risks, conditions and symptoms we haven't received sufficient training for. There are also specific age groups that require additional supervision and training. All of these factors require us to structure our practice and training in a way that effectively and safely meets their needs. It's essential to recognise our limitations and focus on the clients we are best equipped to serve, ensuring we can provide them with effective and secure support.

Now that you are clear on the ideal clients to include in your caseload, let's explore the options to generate referrals for your practice to align with your professional goals and values to build a thriving caseload that reflects your aspirations and vision for your practice.

Begin With Your Clients in Mind

The first questions you asked yourself were, 'Who do I want to work with and who do I not?' Beyond this, it's important to put yourself in the mind of the clients you want to work with. When looking for a therapist, here are several factors they might consider:

- The therapist's therapeutic approach and their qualifications
- The clinical schedule the therapist works
- Location, in relation to their home if they are looking for face-to-face sessions
- Whether the therapist is associated with their insurance company
- Affordability
- How to book an appointment and the onboarding process
- Whether they like the look of the therapist (probably the most common)

It is crucial to make it as straightforward and open as possible for people to reach out and schedule appointments with you. Many individuals seeking therapy are going through tough times and might feel anxious about the process. Deciding on a therapist is a significant choice in terms of time and finances. To assist them on their journey, imagine walking in their shoes, guiding them from when they discover you to when they sit down with you. What information would they find useful? What insights could ease their concerns? Don't forget a friendly homepage on your website with your photo, as people choose therapists they connect with, so a welcoming image can go a long way in building that initial rapport. Provide clear directions, including the correct postcodes and nearest parking. If you provide your services online, a guide to getting the most out of online sessions is a nice touch. People like to see where they are going, so pictures of the therapy room where you work can build familiarity and help people feel more secure, even if they'll only be joining you remotely. Let's explore the options and ways you can generate referrals for your private practice.

Self-funding Clients

Attracting self-funding clients is often seen as the gold-standard referral. Self-funding clients have purposefully chosen to work directly with you. They may have researched you, meaning they know how you work and feel aligned with your mission and values. They likely already feel you are a good fit for them, which is a great starting point for the therapeutic relationship. Working with clients who are engaged and committed to working with you is very rewarding. When no third party is involved, you can focus on the client's needs rather than a third party's requirements and reduce paperwork demands.

Rather than having a set amount of sessions, you and the client decide the number of sessions required with the support of the therapeutic formulation. Self-funding clients pay you directly, and you will get paid on the day, improving cash flow. I've found that self-referring clients may return at other points in their lives if they have had a good therapeutic experience with you and are more likely to recommend you, positively impacting your client base.

The downside of working with self-referring clients is that it initially requires a financial and time investment to create the visibility for self-referring clients to find you.

When starting out in private practice, you often can't wait long for referrals to come through and finances can be limited until you start seeing clients. It took approximately three months from setting up my website to getting my first self-referral. There are a few shortcuts I now know about, which will be shared in Chapter 6 on websites, but you should prepare for it to take time to build up your caseload. Some therapists notice more referral fluctuations when working with self-referring clients, such as during holiday periods this can be managed by having a short waiting list. Once you have a steady stream of referrals, you can offer people other therapists to refer on to or to be placed on a waiting list, in my experience I've found people will wait 4–8 weeks for sessions but no longer generally.

Word of Mouth

This is where your happy and satisfied clients shout about their positive therapy experience with you and recommend your private practice to their friends, family, colleagues or social media followers. This positive feedback will attract new clients to your business and help you build your reputation and establish your expertise in your field, making it even more likely that new clients will choose to work with you. The benefits are that it is cost-effective as it's free, establishes trust quickly with your new clients and positively impacts the therapeutic relationship. The difficulty is that it takes time. I was a year into my private practice before I noticed word-of-mouth referrals coming to me. One way to encourage this kind of referral is to ask and mention you have space to take on new clients. It's surprising how many people assume you are busy when you might not be.

Testimonials

Testimonials are written or spoken statements from satisfied clients that describe their positive therapy experience with you. While the stigma around therapy is declining, some individuals still prefer to keep their therapy journeys private. Understandably, not everyone may be comfortable granting permission to share even an anonymous testimonial. To gather these valuable endorsements, seeking feedback at the end of therapy sessions is a good practice. This helps you in your self-reflection and provides an opening to request an anonymous testimonial that can benefit your business. Over time, you'll accumulate a treasure trove of such testimonials, serving as persuasive social proof for potential clients and showcasing the effectiveness and quality of your service.

Networking

Networking is the process of building relationships with other individuals, professionals or therapists that will help you grow your caseload. Networking can take many forms, such as attending professional events and conferences, joining local business groups and professional associations, collaborating with other professionals, utilising social media groups and helping answer questions on forums while letting people know you are available. Hosting a podcast has also allowed me to reach out and connect with many incredible people, including fellow therapists, and get to know them, as listeners get an to enjoy some conversations and interviews that help them understand more about the world of therapy.

Networking is a useful part of building a successful private practice as a therapist. By connecting with other professionals and building relationships, you can expand your client base, establish your reputation as an expert in your field and build a supportive network of colleagues who can help you grow and develop your practice. One of the most useful things I did when I set up my practice was getting to know therapists in other fields like beauticians, health stores, massage therapists and physiotherapists. They work daily with people who may also struggle with their mental health. They are not in competition with you, and it's helpful for them to have a place to refer their clients. Equally, it's good for you to have a list of people you trust to refer on to if needed. I love trying out different therapies, so I was very authentic in using their services and getting to know them. Building up this kind of network takes time, but it's very rewarding and effective. Make sure to really get to know people; just dropping off your business cards doesn't have the same impact.

Directories

There are two types of directories – professional directories like *Psychology Today*, and counselling directories or business directories; both are popular. This is where you can pay to list your service and they will get your profile in front of people who are actively looking for your services. I used professional directories like *Psychology Today* and the Counselling Directory effectively for the first few years in my business before I had enough momentum for it to happen organically.

Business directories are another effective avenue to enhance your private practice's online visibility and generate more referrals. The sheer multitude of directories available can be overwhelming, which is why services like the Directory Building Service from Pocketsite.co.uk exist to assist you in this endeavour. They will list your business on various reputable directories, saving you time and effort.

By leveraging the power of well-established directories like Yelp and Google Business Profile, you significantly increase the likelihood of potential clients discovering your practice when they search for therapy services in their local area. These platforms have a broad user base actively seeking recommendations and information about various businesses, including therapy providers. You also gain credibility and visibility within your target market by listing your practice on these respected directories. It's also underutilised, as most therapists are unaware of the benefits of using business directories, or neglect to do so as it's time-consuming. Therefore, it will help you stand out from others.

Remember, it is essential to include accurate, up-to-date information about your practice and ensure your profile is consistent across all your platforms so that it's acknowledged as the same business, which is good for reach.

Referral Agencies

When embarking on a private practice journey, exploring opportunities with referral agencies is common, especially if you hold professional accreditation. These agencies act as intermediaries connecting treatment providers like yourself with potential clients or medical/legal organisations seeking therapy services within your area. Upon your registering with these agencies, they will notify you whenever a referral aligns with your expertise and location.

Working with referral agencies offers several advantages. First, it relieves you of the need to actively search for referrals or invest extensively in marketing efforts, saving you valuable time and resources. However, it's worth noting that these agencies often offer lower rates for your services. Additionally, the payment terms and conditions may not be favourable, the paperwork demands can be high and the number of sessions clients can access might be restricted. Email correspondence required by referral agencies can also consume additional hours, further reducing your pay rate. If you decide to pursue this avenue, carefully review all contracts and clarify the data protection responsibilities.

Another drawback is that if another therapist joins the agency or charges lower fees, it can impact the number of referrals you receive, and this will come out of the blue so you won't have time to prepare. I have personally experienced situations where a referral company kept me quite busy, only to experience a sudden decline in referrals. This valuable lesson highlighted the importance of diversifying referral sources to avoid relying too heavily on one agency.

Building a solid working relationship with individuals at the referral agency can be beneficial, but staff turnover may make maintaining such relationships challenging. Some therapists choose to work exclusively with referral agencies due to their network and support, allowing for easy referral communication or the ability to refer a client back if deemed inappropriate. Some agencies specialise in specific client presentations, such as those involved in road traffic accidents, which may appeal to therapists seeking predictable case profiles.

It's essential to remain aware that if the referral agency goes into administration, outstanding debts may not be paid, posing potential financial risks.

If this is a referral avenue you will explore, here is a checklist you can work through to ensure they are a suitable company and that you have all the information required to make an informed decision about whether to work with them.

- Ask what types of referrals you are likely to get from them, how many sessions are offered to clients and what support there is from the referral company.
- Understand the agency's referral process. Clarify how referrals are assigned.
- What is the likely frequency of referrals?
- Research and evaluate the reputation and track record of the referral agency. Look for reviews and feedback from other therapists who have worked with them.
- Are they operating in line with the values of your private practice?
- Ensure you understand the fee structure and that it is reasonable and affordable for your practice.
- Ensure they prioritise client confidentiality and have appropriate measures in place to safeguard client information.
- Ensure you understand the contractual agreement's terms with the referral agency. Are there any restrictions or obligations you need to be aware of?
- Read through their data protection policy and be aware of your obligations.
- Are there any exclusivity clauses?

- How do they assess potential clients before making referrals?
- If a referral is not suitable, what is the process for finding the client a new therapist?
- Look through the report templates to assess the potential workload and ask about the frequency of reports.
- If there are concerns about risk, what support is there?
- What do you do in an emergency? Point of contact? Is there any out-of-hours support?
- Do they provide any case management, supervision or training benefits?

When it comes to referral agencies, it's important to remember their main priority is their own business. As a therapist, you are working with them as a contractor. Therefore, it is crucial to prioritise and protect your own needs. While these agencies can be valuable in connecting you with potential clients, keeping your professional goals, values and boundaries in mind is essential. Take the time to evaluate their terms and conditions, negotiate for fair terms and ensure the agency's expectations align with what you're looking for; you can then establish a mutually beneficial relationship.

Health Insurance Companies

A health insurance company is a business that provides health insurance to individuals, families or groups such as employees. Health insurance covers the cost of medical and surgical expenses incurred by the insured. Health insurance companies collect premiums from policyholders and, in exchange, provide coverage for a wide range of medical costs. The specific benefits and coverage offered by a health insurance company can vary widely depending on the policy, and premiums are often based on factors such as age, health status and the level of coverage desired.

As an accredited therapist, you can register as a healthcare provider with health insurance companies. They will then send you a contract to review. There is sometimes room to negotiate your fees, but often, these companies have fixed rates they will pay. You can register with as many companies as you like. Sometimes, they might put you on a list of therapists and direct their clients to the list, who will contact you from there. But generally, people with health insurance independently look for a therapist local to them and reach out in the same way as a self-referral. There is less paperwork than working with referral agencies, but you still need to have your own platform, such as a website, so that potential clients can find and contact you.

People's policies can change, which could mean the insurance company suddenly stops paying for sessions or may not pay for the first couple of sessions due to excesses on the policy. Having a statement in your therapy contract that says the client is liable for the cost if the insurance company doesn't pay for a session is useful. There will be companies that you find are easy to work with and are reliable and others that are not such a good fit. I'd advise you to register with a few and get to know them.

Working as an Associate

This is where you work under the umbrella of a private company that finds referrals for you. Some clients prefer to see a therapist who works within a larger organisation. These companies take you on as an 'associate.' You remain self-employed, and when the company passes you a referral, they take a cut from what you earn. Effectively, they do all the marketing and work to get the referrals so you don't have to, cutting out the costs and additional work involved. They might also provide administrative support and supervision.

It's important to acknowledge that this set-up may resemble being an employee without job security. Nonetheless, when starting out, this can be an appealing option as it offers a support network, guidance and a ready-made infrastructure. If you are considering this approach, it is advisable to contact other therapists working for the company and enquire about their experiences. Gaining insights from their first-hand perspectives can provide valuable information to inform your decision-making process.

Employer Assistance Program

An Employer Assistance Program (EAP) is a work-based program designed to assist employees in addressing personal challenges that could affect their job performance, health and overall well-being. EAPs are often included in an employer's benefits package. Employees can seek professional help through the EAP, and therapists can benefit from consistent referrals.

EAPs may have specific requirements or expectations for participating therapists, such as specific qualifications, training or certifications. It's crucial to ensure you meet these criteria and are willing to abide by any guidelines set forth by the EAP.

Additionally, the pay rates for EAP referrals are generally low but may vary, so it's important to consider the financial implications of accepting these clients into your practice.

Private Practice Clinics

This is where you choose to work in an environment where other therapists are already established, allowing you to benefit from their existing client base and the potential for cross-referrals. By joining a team of therapists, you gain the advantage of working alongside professionals who have built their businesses and established client networks. This can provide a valuable opportunity for collaboration and learning from experienced practitioners. Being part of such an environment offers several benefits. First, you can tap into the reputation and credibility of the established therapists, which can enhance your own professional standing. Clients who seek therapy may feel more comfortable and confident knowing they are accessing services within a trusted practice. Second, there is the potential for cross-referrals among therapists within the same practice. When clients have specific needs or preferences that align better with another therapist's expertise, they can be seamlessly referred to the appropriate colleague. This benefits the clients and fosters a sense of teamwork and cooperation among therapists. Working in an environment with other therapists also provides a support network that can be invaluable, allowing for professional growth and development, as you can exchange ideas, seek guidance and learn from the experiences of your colleagues.

Additionally, the shared administrative responsibilities and resources within the practice can alleviate some of the burdens of running a solo private practice. It is important to note that while joining an established practice can offer numerous advantages, there are a few things to consider. You will need to assess the compatibility of your therapeutic approach and values with the existing practice, ensuring the work environment and culture align with your professional goals, vision, values and ethical standards.

Social Media

At a recent online event, I asked 300 delegates to answer this question – if they were to find a therapist, what would be their first step? There were two popular answers: first, ask a friend, and second, go to Google.

However, I see many therapists pouring most of their energy into social media. While I have gained some referrals through social media, it has never been my primary objective. Instead, I utilise social media to drive traffic to my website and create brand awareness, allowing potential clients to get to know me and my work.

My primary concern with social media is the significant time investment required to consistently generate engaging content with a limited lifespan. Trying to figure out the various algorithms can be exhausting, especially when it feels like they are constantly moving the goalposts.

Social media platforms focus on keeping people on their platforms for as long as possible. This is beneficial for generating advertising revenue, and this is how they make money, which is their priority; it's not helping you promote your business. Other platforms like Substack are doing things differently; this is where we host the Therapist Corner community. Substack has no algorithm or advertising; they do well if you do well, and if you want to take all your followers to another platform, then you can, as they allow you to download your community's email addresses as you own them, all of which is a refreshing change. Hopefully, more of these platforms will emerge.

If you're unsure about social media, I'd advise you to use only platforms you enjoy and that align with your business values, and somewhere your potential clients are likely to want to hang out too.

Building an engaged audience on social media demands substantial time and effort, especially given that algorithms frequently change the game's rules; we will cover audience building in greater depth in the final chapter. It is important to recognise that social media platforms are owned by someone else and, as a user, you have limited control over them. While they may work well for you currently, the landscape can change instantly, potentially impacting your ability to reach your audience effectively. This happened a few years ago on Facebook, when Mark Zuckerberg no longer supported the reach of Facebook business pages. Overnight, thousands of businesses lost out and had a significant reduction in reach, and therefore revenue, without any warning.

In contrast, having your own website provides a more stable and controllable platform. It serves as your digital home, where you have full ownership and control over your content and online presence. You own all the hard work you put into it and it will continue to serve you for many years.

Social media platforms can supplement your online presence, but weighing the time and effort required against the potential benefits is important. Consider a balanced approach, where you prioritise building your website as a central hub for your online presence and while utilising social media as a supplementary tool for brand awareness and community engagement. By establishing a solid foundation on your platform, you can maintain control over your online presence and adapt to changes in the digital landscape more effectively.

Paid Advertising

In addition to social media and having your own website, utilising Google or Facebook advertising can be a powerful strategy to drive traffic to your website and improve its search engine optimisation (SEO). Advertising through these platforms can help accelerate the building of your online authority, particularly when you have a new website, resulting in more people finding your practice and ultimately increasing the number of referrals you receive.

However, it's important to approach online advertising with caution. Without a solid understanding of how to effectively manage campaigns, spending a significant amount of money without achieving the desired results is possible. It may be beneficial to enlist the expertise of professionals who are knowledgeable in online advertising to help you set up and optimise your campaigns. Hiring someone with expertise in this area can maximise the return on your investment and ensure your advertising efforts align with your goals; however, the costs increase.

Investing in your own understanding of online advertising can also be valuable. By gaining a good degree of knowledge in this field, you can prevent companies from taking advantage of you and ensure you are making informed decisions regarding your advertising budget. Consider investing in training or consultation to develop your skills and understanding of effective advertising strategies.

Conclusion

We have explored many pathways you can choose for generating referrals, setting the stage for you to establish a robust and resilient caseload. To ensure that the options you choose align with the values and goals of your private practice, ask yourself: Who do I want to work with? Who would benefit most from my services? Who do I NOT want to work with? Avoid the 'Scattergun Method' of registering everywhere. Let your answers guide your approach to seeking the right referral sources for you to work with, and don't place all your referral source eggs in one basket!

While being an exceptional therapist will eventually lead to word-of-mouth recommendations, the ultimate gold standard in referrals, initially, you must focus on becoming visible to potential clients. They need to find you and understand how to work with you. As the demand for therapy is steadily growing, so are the opportunities; your task is to create the right environment for the right clients to discover you.

You can invest in building your visibility and referrals independently or opt to work with companies that handle this aspect for you, often in exchange for a portion of your pay. Don't forget to be vigilant about reviewing the terms and conditions of referral agencies, ensuring they work for you, and regularly monitor and evaluate the effectiveness of your referral sources, ensuring the growth and stability of your private practice.

Remembering that what works wonders for one therapist may not yield the same results for another is vital. There's no one-size-fits-all approach. If, for instance, you loathe social media, don't force yourself to use it. Instead, create a business that resonates with your uniqueness, and you'll find yourself nurturing a practice you genuinely love.

Lastly, if your goal is to work with more self-funding clients, you must learn the art of saying no to the referrals you'd prefer to avoid, making room for the ones you desire. Additionally, adopt a well-defined marketing strategy, which we'll delve into in the next chapter.

Business Plan Actions

Decide who you want to work with and where your referrals will come from, using the templates shown in Figures 4.1–4.5, and then you'll know where to put your energy and efforts.

BUSINESS PLANNING QUESTIONS

WHO DO YOU WANT TO WORK WITH?

WHO DO YOU NOT WANT TO WORK WITH?

Figure 4.1 Building a caseload 1: Write out the types of clients you would like to work with and those you won't.

SELECT REFERRAL SOURCES

- SELF-FUNDING CLIENTS ☐   • SOCIAL MEDIA ☐
- NETWORKING ☐   • PAID ADVERTISING ☐
- DIRECTORIES PROFESSIONAL ☐   • PRIVATE PRACTICE CLINICS ☐
- BUSINESS DIRECTORIES ☐
- EMPLOYER ASSISTANCE
  PROGRAMME ☐
- REFERRAL AGENCIES ☐
- HEALTH INSURANCE
  COMPANIES ☐

Figure 4.2 Building a caseload 2: List the referral sources you will focus on working with.

BUSINESS PLANNING ACTION

CREATE YOUR SHORT TERM PLAN

Figure 4.3 Building a caseload 3: Create your short-term plan.

BUSINESS PLANNING ACTION

CREATE YOUR MID-TERM PLAN

Figure 4.4 Building a caseload 4: Create your mid-term plan.

BUSINESS PLANNING ACTION

CREATE YOUR LONG TERM PLAN

Figure 4.5 Building a caseload 5: Create your long-term plan.

Chapter 5

Marketing Your Practice

If referrals are the life source of your private practice, marketing is the magic behind each referral. It's all the things you do to make your practice more visible, letting potential clients know about your services and attracting the right clients to your therapy offerings.

Have you ever felt uncomfortable with the idea of marketing your therapeutic services? You're not alone. The unease comes from a place of integrity; therapists are dedicated to ethical practice and cringe at the thought of employing pushy, salesy tactics that might lure individuals into unsuitable services. But what if marketing could be different? What if it could be a force for good? Simon Sinek challenged us in 2009 to see beyond the manipulative gimmicks of price slashes and flashy promotions. He taught us that true motivation comes from inspiration, not manipulation.

Imagine marketing that strikes a chord with the very heart of why you became a therapist – to help, to heal, to connect. What if your marketing efforts could echo these noble aspirations, aligning with the beliefs and values that you and your potential clients hold dear? This isn't about selling – it's about starting a conversation, building a community and reaching out to those who are already seeking the kind of profound change you can facilitate.

When we infuse our marketing with the same authenticity and care we give to our therapy, we transform it. It becomes a bridge, extending the reach of your helping hands to those silently pleading for guidance. Isn't that a form of therapy in itself? Let's redefine marketing in therapy, not as a necessary evil, but as an opportunity to inspire and invite meaningful engagement. After all, your services are not just another commodity; they are a lifeline for many. Shouldn't your message reflect that?

This chapter aims to turn everything you know about marketing on its head and provide a new approach for you to enjoy and embrace it. You will market your private practice from a place of service to potential clients who need help finding the right support and therapist for them. It is possible to do this in a way that is aligned with your values. You can be part of the changing landscape where people have more knowledge of the different mental health support options open to them and understand how they can find the right therapist.

DOI: 10.4324/9781003401391-6

Currently, there needs to be more understanding of the different types of therapy and clarity around people's qualifications and accreditations. For example, it's common to meet clients who have had a difficult experience trying to find therapists to work with, or clients who think they have had a course of CBT but later learn that the therapist's training was limited to a one-day taster course. This is unfair, and you can be part of correcting this unethical marketing so that people can make educated and informed choices about their mental heal. The sad thing is that when people are distressed and eager to find help, they can be more vulnerable and fall prey to this type of marketing.

On a positive note, the rise of online communication, testimonials and reviews expose dirty tactics. However, we still have some way to go. I've seen therapists criticise other therapy models and claim theirs is the best, or vilify medication and say therapy is the only answer. They are trying to tap into people's anxiety to draw them in. What values are they aligning themselves with, I wonder, if any?

Thankfully, many potential clients will see through this technique and quite rightly not go near these therapists.

> During her speech at the 2016 Democratic National Convention, First Lady Michelle Obama said, 'When they go low, we go high' (Obama, 2016).
>
> The quote calls for people to conduct themselves to a higher standard in the face of adversity and encourages maintaining a high moral and ethical standard even when confronted with low or unfair tactics.

This chapter is split into two sections. The first focuses on the 'what is' and 'how to' of marketing. The second section is written by Sophie A. Wood, who, along with creating websites, is a graphic designer; she helps people build their brand. Sophie will walk you through the essentials of branding, including the choice of colours and fonts, all the way to designing a website that captures the true spirit of your brand's personality.

Figure 5.1 shows a visual diagram of how branding and marketing overlap; Humberstone (2017) states that 'an effective brand is a beautiful blend of strategy and creativity.'

By the end of this chapter, you'll have a deeper understanding of marketing in a way that aligns with your values and the role branding plays in your overall marketing strategy, setting your business apart from others so the clients who need you can find you.

Marketing Is Not . . .

- About tricking people to come and see you for therapy.
- About overpromising and under-delivering.
- About giving the impression you are one thing when you are another.

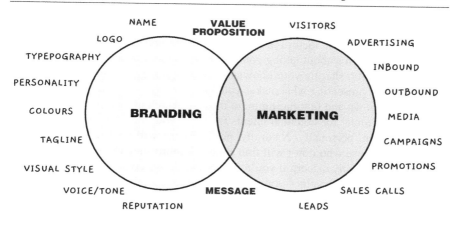

Figure 5.1 Marketing and branding.

Marketing Is . . .

- About helping potential clients make an informed decision about who they see for therapy.
- About making sure the clients who walk through your door are a good fit for you and that you have the right knowledge and skills to support them.

Marketing your practice is an integral part of the service you provide to your clients. In his book, *The 1-Page Marketing Plan*, Allan Dib (2016) provides this straightforward explanation of what marketing is:

> If the circus is coming to town and you paint a sign saying, 'Circus Coming to the Showground on Saturday,' that's *advertising*.
>
> If you put that sign on the back of an elephant and walk it into town, that's *promotion*.
>
> If the elephant walks through the mayor's flower bed and the local newspaper writes a story about it, that's *publicity*.
>
> And if you get the mayor to laugh about it, that's *public relations*.
>
> If the town citizens go to the circus, you show them the many entertainment booths, explain how much fun they'll have spending money at the booths, answer their questions and ultimately, they spend a lot at the circus, that's *sales*.
>
> And if you planned the whole thing, that's *marketing*.

It's as simple as that! Marketing is the strategy you create to promote your private practice so potential clients can get to know who you are, like what you do and trust you enough to want to have therapy with you.

Know, Like, Trust

The 'Know, Like, Trust' factor is a cornerstone in marketing, but what exactly does it mean? Initially, it's about letting potential clients get to 'Know' you. This step is all about visibility: sharing your knowledge, highlighting your unique qualities as a therapist, and presenting what makes you different. Your marketing should aim to make you a known and familiar figure to those in search of therapy.

Next, it's crucial for potential clients to 'Like' you, meaning you need to resonate with them personally. Naturally, not everyone will connect with you, and that's okay – those who don't will find someone more suited to them. Your job is to help clients swiftly discern if you're the right fit. This could be through the way you communicate, the values you stand for, or the empathy you display for their challenges. Your marketing efforts should make them feel heard and supported.

Finally, and most importantly, is the 'Trust' factor. Trust is the cornerstone of any therapeutic relationship. Your marketing should convey reliability, professionalism and the effectiveness of your therapy services. You can convey this through having a consistent brand and a consistent marketing strategy, so you show up as you say you will. When potential clients trust you, they believe that you can help them, and they are more likely to choose you as their therapist.

Finally, and most importantly, is the 'Trust' factor. Trust is the cornerstone of any therapeutic relationship. The brand you create, and your marketing efforts, need to breathe reliability and professionalism and speak to the success of your therapeutic approach. You do this by being consistent in your branding and marketing rhythm, showing up just as you promise. When clients sense your trustworthiness, they start to believe in your ability to help them, and that's when they're truly ready to take the step to work with you. We can often overcomplicate ideas or share psychological jargon with an aim of impressing people but when you confuse you lose, simplicity is key

> Being able to simplify an idea and successfully share it with others is both the path to understanding it and the proof that you do. One of the ways we mask our lack of understanding of any idea is by using more words, bigger words and less necessary words.
>
> Steven Bartlett (2023)

In summary, marketing for your private practice is not just about visibility. It's a strategic process that guides potential clients through getting to know you, liking what you represent and ultimately trusting you enough to engage in therapy with you.

Do you have the Know/Like/Trust factor?

When you are marketing your private practice, potential clients will book an appointment with you when they . . .

1. Know who you are.
2. Like what you do.
3. Trust you can deliver it.

How do you go about building the Know/Like/Trust factor? Through the use of marketing tools or drivers, such as website content, social media posts, guest blogging, podcasting, video content and profiles on directories. These create visibility so people can get to know you, establish that they like you and build trust in your ability to help them. A marketing strategy is the planning behind these marketing drivers.

Imagine you were going to build a house. Can you order a pile of bricks and just start laying them? No – you'd end up with a mess. So, what do you do? You hire an architect and a builder. They plan everything so you have a big picture or vision of what you want your house to look like.

If you have done the work in earlier chapters, you have already begun to understand your 'why' and build a clear mission and vision for your practice. You know what you stand for, and you have your values in place. Therefore, you are well on your way to getting to know your private practice, and the more precise you are, the more evident it will be in your messaging and for others to understand. The next step is to hone in on who your practice will serve.

Niche Your Practice

In the early days of my private practice, the fear of empty appointment books led me down the path of the 'Scattergun Method,' a desperate plea to cast my net wide in hopes of catching anyone and everyone. Yet, as and Mares so aptly stated in 2015, 'attempting to create a service 'that appeals to everyone' is destined 'to end up appealing to no one.' And that's exactly what happened. My all-encompassing, generic messaging was a whisper lost in the noise of choices, resonating with no one.

I learned that this pitfall isn't just mine; it's seen in the long, overwhelming lists on therapists' websites, where they lay out an array of services, credentials and treatable conditions. This barrage of information may seem thorough but often leaves potential clients dazed and more lost than when they started their search.

The revelation came when I shifted my strategy, and I began to speak directly to the heart of a singular client's experience rather than broadcasting to a faceless crowd. Initially, I was concerned that by narrowing my focus, I might limit my practice. However, it turned out to be quite the opposite. By zeroing in on a specific message, I was able to connect more deeply with those seeking exactly what I offer. This precision didn't just shrink my audience; it clarified my voice and drew in those who needed my expertise the most. The result was a practice bustling with the right clients and the individuals I am truly passionate about helping and can have the greatest impact working with.

I built a new website with my ideal client/community in mind. It was a completely different experience. I also really enjoyed putting it together. Has it worked? Absolutely! I've also seen it work for other therapists I've coached, such as Sheena, 'The Pain Therapist'; who has done a fantastic job of nailing her niche. I know that I consistently attract my ideal clients because they tell me arriving at my website feels like coming home. This has made me more determined to continue building my business with them, and only them, in mind. However, I also attract a much broader client base. For example, the ideal client I had in mind when I created my website was female, but I've consistently had a 50/50 mix of female and male clients. It never prevents clients from coming to see you unless they are not the right fit for you. Niching provides clarity.

> Niche – 'relating to or aimed at a small group of people with particular interests or needs niche products/markets.'
> *Cambridge Business English Dictionary* (2021).

Niching demonstrates a confident approach, and this builds trust with clients. It will help your business become more effective and can set the stage for further growth. It doesn't necessarily mean you'll only work within this one niche forever, but it allows you to focus your brand and develop your voice. Knowing and understanding your niche is also useful when working with others in your business, such as designers, copywriters and virtual assistants.

Creating content is so much easier when you know who you're communicating with. In marketing, people will talk about having an ideal client in mind, which is useful, but we need to expand this further and be inclusive about the community your ideal client is in and the diversity of this community. For example, if you use pictures on your website, are they representative of all the diversity in your niche? Some businesses will have someone review their business from an inclusive, cultural and diversity perspective yearly to help reduce the unconscious biases we can hold. I've had this done, and it's so valuable and eye-opening.

Approaches to Finding Your Niche

There are various ways to niche your private practice. You can choose to focus on the type of therapy you provide or a specific condition you treat, such as anxiety, pain, or trauma. Alternatively, consider the clients you enjoy working with and those who get the most out of your therapy. Ask yourself who they are and what they do. What help do they need? What are their struggles? You'll likely find some common threads among the answers to these questions. Bring these elements together to create a picture of your ideal client and the diversity of their community.

Questions to Consider

> - Do you have an area of expertise or a particular area of interest?
> - What are your key skills?
> - Who are the clients you have most enjoyed working with?
> - Which clients enjoy working with you?
> - Are there clients or presentations you enjoy working with less?
> - What will your ideal client be looking for in a therapist?
> - What is important to them?
> - What are their biggest struggles?
> - What would they search for on Google?
> - Where will they spend time online?
> - What magazines do they read, or what podcasts do they listen to?
> - What are their demographics?

The goal of this exercise is for you to become VERY clear about who you are serving and what you can do for them. When creating every aspect of your business, you should have this person in your mind's eye and heart. Doing this will attract the people who love what you do and are looking for your service.

> Don't forget to define the group of people that make up the community you are committed to working with. By specifying your ideal community, you are giving yourself more room to envision people of different races, religions, ages, disabilities and sexual orientations. Help people feel seen, valued and welcomed.

Marketing Strategy

In today's digital age, it's more important than ever to ensure your business is visible to customers. Having an effective strategy in place will set you apart. It will also keep you consistent because you'll know what you need to do and when. Consistency plays a vital role in building trust with your audience. How you show up online also demonstrates how you will show up in therapy. With so many businesses vying for attention online, getting lost in the shuffle can be easy. That's why having a strong online presence is crucial, making it easy for potential clients to find you and learn more about what you offer. The marketing strategy you create is the roadmap for how your potential clients can get to know who you are, like what you do and trust you enough to want to come and see you and have their therapy with you. It maps through the full therapeutic journey with you, from how they find you online to how you discharge them from your service.

A 10-Stage Marketing Strategy

1. *Who:* Who are your ideal clients? Create a detailed client persona to understand their needs, the communities they live in and their challenges. Why would they be looking for a therapist?

2. *Where:* Understanding how clients find you is key. Think about how they might search for a therapist; where they would look? Are they using Google, Facebook groups, LinkedIn, or Instagram? Do they engage with blogs or podcasts? Your visibility in these spaces is essential for connection. These platforms drive traffic to your main platform, generally your website. Always track how new enquiries find you to gauge the effectiveness of your marketing efforts and focus on the most successful strategies.

3. *Messaging:* What do they need to know, believe or understand to decide you are the right therapist? You need to convey the information that demonstrates you're the right therapist for them. Clearly express your values, mission and vision. You are communicating the unique advantages of your therapeutic methods and approach relevant to their specific challenges.

4. *Main platform:* This is the main place clients need to arrive at to begin working with you. Generally, this will be your website. You will use your marketing drivers to attract people to your website. Ensure it's user-friendly, easy to navigate, informative and reflective of your professional brand. If the main aim of your platform is for people to book an appointment, it needs to be clear how they can do this on every page they arrive on.

5. *The enquiry:* Have a straightforward process for managing queries in a timely, efficient manner. This includes sending immediate acknowledgements, sending the person who enquires useful information, like blog posts or information about the therapy you provide to help them decide if this is the right step for them, and ensuring they know how to take the next step of booking an appointment.

6. *The onboarding:* When booking the initial session, what information do they need for their first session to go as smoothly as possible? What information do you need to set up their file and start the process?

7. *The delivery:* Where will you deliver therapy – online, or face-to-face? Create a therapeutic space and ensure the therapy delivery is of the highest quality. What resources and materials will you provide? How can people contact you in between sessions? Have clear policies and processes in place.

8. *The discharge:* Set up a clear process and establish what information clients will take away with them. This is also the time to ask for feedback and testimonials and ask them to share your service with others. Word of mouth is the gold standard in marketing.

9. *Consistency:* This is central to the effectiveness of a marketing strategy. Decide how much time you can invest each month into marketing your business, plan it and stick to it.

10. *Review and measure:* Review and measure the impact of your efforts by tracking key performance indicators (KPIs) like website traffic, enquiry rates,

conversion rates, engagement on social media and return on investment (ROI). Use this data to refine your strategy, ensuring your marketing remains effective and aligned with your business goals.

Marketing Drivers

With your strategy in place, you now need to consider the drivers you will use to create visibility and drive potential clients to your website (or the main platform from which people can work with you). With your ideal client in mind, consider where they will be hanging out online and how you can get your practice visible to them.

Here are some ideas:

- Search engine optimisation (SEO)
- Writing blog posts
- Building communities – Facebook groups, Substack, memberships
- Paid advertising
- Creating videos – for social media or your website
- Social media and social ads
- Testimonials
- Directory listings
- Podcasting
- Signage
- Delivering workshops
- Public speaking and presenting
- Writing guest posts/articles for magazines
- Being a guest on podcasts
- Email lists – discussed more in Chapter 11

These all require an investment of either time or money. Decide which is best for you; eventually, the costs will reduce once you have created the momentum and a foundation of content.

Some of the drivers will have what's called a 'long tail.' This means they can create visibility for a very long time. Examples include podcasting, videos and blogging. Other drivers will have a 'short tail' – for example, a social media post that is only visible for a few hours. When creating content, I'd always recommend using a mixture, but the harder you can make your content work for you, the better. For example, if you write a blog post, you could use parts of this content for social media posts. This is called repurposing and maximising your efforts.

If you are considering building a business on a social media platform as your primary platform, keep in mind that while it is a great way to be visible – and most people expect you to have a social media presence – somebody else owns the platform and can change the rules anytime, impacting your business. In contrast, your website is your own platform, so I'd always recommend that this is where you spend most of your investment and utilise social media as a driver to your own platform.

I work with some therapists who don't enjoy social media. If you resonate with this, it's probable that social media marketing may neither play to your strengths nor spark your creativity in your spare time. Committing extra effort in an area you don't enjoy is unsustainable. I believe in building a business that you're passionate about, as that passion is contagious and can draw others to love what you do as well.

For many years my focus has been creating a blog post for my website and then using a few sections of the blog for social media posts. What I wrote five years ago still creates visibility for me now. Occasionally, I spend 10 minutes updating it, or adding a new image, and it's like a whole new piece of content. The key is to be consistent in whatever you plan to do. It can take 3–6 months for your marketing efforts to begin to reward you in referrals, so it's a long game, but when you have consistency, you will soon have momentum.

Creating Content

If you decide to invest some time in creating content, here are a few tips. First, don't compromise quality over quantity with social media posts. If you only have one hour a month to focus on social media, then that's all you have, but it's essential that you plan it in. Having a steady stream of self-funding clients is not about luck; it's about having a simple, easy-to-follow content strategy that keeps you focused and your messaging clear and consistent. Instead of rushing to create content at the last minute, you'll have the time and headspace to produce high-quality, engaging posts. Your messaging will have more clarity, it will fit with your goals and values, and you can create a flow of work that makes sense to the people following you. Planning also saves time and reduces stress, as it allows for bulk content creation and scheduling.

It can feel scary to put yourself out there and be visible. To overcome this, always begin with your client in mind. What do they need to know, learn or understand to work with you? The content you create allows people to make an informed choice.

For many therapists, not knowing where to start or what to write is one of the main blocks to creating content. Here are some ideas to get you started:

- *The introductory post:* Make a memorable first impression with an introductory post. It's like a virtual handshake that introduces you to potential clients and helps them understand who you are and what you do.
- *Appointment availability post:* If you have slots to fill, let people know. Otherwise, they might presume you are busy when you actually have space.
- *Know/Like/Trust post:* What do clients need to know, learn or understand to work with you? Think about each element and create content around this, including your 'why,' mission, vision, and values.
- *Personal story post:* Share a brief, relatable story that illustrates your passion for therapy and your journey to becoming a therapist. This humanises your practice and allows readers to connect with you on a personal level.

- *Delight and Excite post:* We all love celebrating with people or getting excited about a new venture, so share your wins and what's coming. If you are excited to do some new training, share it and let others join in with you.
- *Expertise and specialisations post:* Highlight your areas of expertise and the specific populations or issues you specialise in. This will help potential clients understand how you can help them and establish your credibility as a therapist.
- *Testimonial post:* Highlight success stories and the testimonials your clients have provided to you (with consent, of course). This illustrates the positive impact therapy can have on individuals' lives. It also helps destigmatise mental health treatment and creates a sense of trust.
- *Transformation post:* People are often looking for a change or a transformation. Can you get them to where they want to be? What is the transformation, and how can you help them?
- *Behind-the-scenes post:* Offer a glimpse into your therapy practice by sharing behind-the-scenes content. This can include photos or videos of your office, a description of your therapeutic approach or a snapshot of your workspace. Humanising your practice fosters connection.
- *Relevant news and research:* Whatever is in the current news will be popular, so share your take on it. This showcases your commitment to staying informed and helps position you as a knowledgeable resource. Don't forget to keep up to date with the upcoming awareness days.
- *Book Club:* People love a book recommendation! Share the books you are reading or recommending to your clients. The same goes for relevant podcasts, films or TV programs.
- *Inspirational and motivational content:* Share motivational quotes, affirmations or uplifting messages to inspire and encourage your audience. These posts can provide a much-needed boost and remind individuals of the importance of mental well-being.

Content Tip

Still trying to figure out what to write about? Use this technique. After each client you see in clinic this week, write down what blog post or book they would find most useful. Was there one thing in the session they found particularly helpful, such as a piece of advice, a strategy or a tip? Jot it down and use this for your content. If it's useful for them, others will want to know about it too.

Creating 'content buckets,' 'pillars' or 'categories' for the different topics you want to cover can help you organise and plan your social media content effectively. By diversifying your content, you engage a broader range of individuals and provide valuable information to your audience. Identifying the key themes you want to write about also makes it easier to develop relevant ideas. Here are some content bucket ideas to consider:

- *Therapy:* You can write about different modalities, explain how therapy works, describe the process and address frequently asked questions.
- *Mental health:* You can provide general advice or tips, write about specific issues and address mental health topics in the news.
- *Your niche:* You can write about a disorder-specific area (such as anxiety or depression) or a strategy (like exposure).

Write and create with your clients in mind and what they most need from you, and you will never be lost for content ideas.

Branding

Branding plays a crucial role when it comes to marketing your business. It involves creating a unique identity for your practice that differentiates it from your competitors in the marketplace. Humberstone (2017) states that 'A well-crafted brand should whisper to your dream clients, intimately and powerfully, communicating that you understand them.'

This is done by developing a brand name, design, symbol, and other features that are easily recognisable and resonate with your ideal clients. Branding is much more than just creating a logo or a catchy tagline. It's about building a consistent, memorable image for your business that resonates with your potential clients.

Effective branding helps to build trust and credibility and creates a lasting impression in the minds of your audience. To create a successful brand, it is important to first have clarity on the values, mission and ideal clients for your private practice. With this information, you can develop a brand strategy that aligns with your business goals and values and resonates with your clients.

> Creating a strong brand involves more than just visual appeal; it's about fostering an emotional connection with your audience. It's about creating an emotional connection between you, your business and your customer. Capturing the essence of what you do and communicating that through every design decision you make for your brand and tapping into the overwhelming majority of customers who buy with their hearts and not their heads.
>
> Fiona Humberstone (2017)

What Is a Brand?

When we get to know someone, we form a perception or idea of them – we 'brand' them. Based on their appearance, behaviour around us and things we hear about them, we start to act, think, and feel a certain way about them. Our relationship with the products and services we interact with every day influences our feelings and opinions about them. This is what we call a brand. The set of ideas a company/product stands for in people's minds.

Anatomy of a Brand

Your brand represents the identity of your practice. A successful brand is one that can create a loyal client base and maintain a positive reputation in the market. To achieve this, a brand should have a clear message and values that resonate with its target audience. Humberstone (2017) shares that 'your brand is a storyteller, and it's the depth of the story that inspires loyalty and engagement.'

It should also have a consistent visual identity and a strong brand personality that sets it apart from its competitors. Another key brand element is its ability to adapt to changing times and trends. A brand is made up of the following elements:

- *Brand strategy:* How do you want your practice to be perceived? What is the demographic, what makes your practice unique and what do you stand for – your mission, vision and values.
- *Brand identity:* This includes:
  - Logo
  - Colours
  - Typography
  - Illustration
  - Photography
  - Graphic elements
  - Tone of voice

The Psychology of Colour

Colour psychology is the study of how colour influences perceptions and behaviours. 'Colour psychology is the science and art of using color in design and branding to influence mood, behaviour and decision-making' (Humberstone, 2017).

The impact of colour can be subtle and largely subconscious, yet it can significantly affect the choices we make every day. From a marketing perspective, understanding colour psychology is essential for creating successful branding and advertising strategies.

Different colours can elicit different psychological responses. For instance, blue is often associated with calmness, stability and reliability, making it a popular choice for corporate brands. Red can elicit feelings of excitement or urgency, which is why it's often used for clearance sales. Green is often linked with nature and tranquillity, and it can also signify growth and renewal. Yellow is associated with happiness and energy but can also be overwhelming if overused.

However, it's important to note that personal, cultural and situational factors can also influence how colours are perceived. For example, while white often signifies purity and simplicity in Western cultures, it can symbolise mourning in some Eastern cultures.

The colours you use for your private practice need to reflect how you want your clients to feel when they land on your platforms or find your content.

A Style Guide for Your Practice

Think of a brand style guide as the 'secret sauce' to maintaining the consistency of your practice's identity. It's far more than mere aesthetics. It's a playbook that delineates your brand's visual and verbal communication. This includes everything from the logo, colour palette, typography, and imagery, to the tone of voice used in the content. A well-defined style guide ensures every interaction resonates with your clients, reinforcing your brand's message and values. It's a vital tool in not just creating, but also nurturing a loyal client base, bolstering your practice's positive reputation in the marketplace.

A comprehensive brand style guide typically includes the following elements:

- *Brand story:* This includes the brand's mission, vision, and values, encapsulating what your practice stands for and its unique positioning in the market.
- *Logo usage:* Guidelines on how the logo should be used, including its variations, minimum size, safe space and inappropriate usage.
- *Colour palette:* Details of the primary and secondary colours that represent your brand.
- *Typography:* Guidelines for typefaces to be used in different circumstances, including primary and secondary fonts, their sizes, line heights, letter spacing, etc.
- *Imagery:* This can include photography, illustrations and iconography, with instructions on their usage to ensure a consistent visual language.
- *Tone of voice:* Describes how your brand communicates with potential clients. This could range from professional and formal to friendly and informal.
- *Social media guidelines:* Specifications for how the brand should appear on various social media platforms.
- *Dos and don'ts:* A clear list of things that should be avoided to maintain brand consistency.

It provides guidelines for maintaining consistency and coherence in your brand's written and visual communication. It is important to remember that the style guide is not a set of rigid rules, but rather a framework that allows for flexibility while still maintaining a cohesive brand identity. It is a living document that should be updated as your brand evolves and grows.

Finding Your Personal Branding Strategy

The first step in branding and marketing yourself is to consider how you want to present yourself. Many businesses either lack a visual identity or have a poorly designed one. In the end, most people will need help understanding or remembering what you do, but you need them to associate a simple idea with your name or company. Your personal brand helps in this space. You are looking to create a mental note in your ideal client's mind with your brand.

Your ideal client will want to know they are working with a professional, especially in the healthcare space where sensitive personal information is readily shared between the client and you. Your personal brand encompasses many small things, and these things are seen by potential clients when deciding whether to work with you. The more consistent your message and image are across all these small things, the easier it is for a client to decide you are the right therapist for them. Your personal brand will seep into all the activities and marketing tools you use, such as your business name, tagline, logo, colours, website, social media accounts, directory listings and images associated with your business.

To work out your personal brand, take a blank piece of paper and look inward to describe yourself, what you offer, your best traits, how your business uses these traits, why you chose this business, and why you are good at it. Your personal brand is about being clear about what you offer and conveying that message to your ideal client's vision. While a brand image is important, your brand must be backed with substance and value. People seeking a therapist are looking for someone they can talk to and trust, so the more you get your personality across, the better.

After documenting your brand strategy, the next step is to approach a branding agency or graphic design agency. Pricing can vary from as little as £100 to £1500K+ for a small business. Using a professional service means you'll get a cohesive brand and style guide that details how the brand can be used. As mentioned earlier, a brand is more than just your logo, and using a professional service means you'll get a brand that can be used across the many platforms now available for marketing your practice.

- Business cards
- Stationery
- Signage
- Web design (desktop/mobile/tablet)
- Social media
- Presentations
- Newsletters
- Email signatures

A Word on Logos

There's a misconception that a logo needs to have some form of a graphic element with it – text only is an option. Rather than overly complicating a message and forcing something, very often with logos, keeping it simple is the best approach. A company name appropriately typeset can work just as effectively and, in some cases, more effectively than combining with different graphic/clip art elements.

Above all, it should be unique, confident, and bold. It should be timeless – which is why it's best to avoid trends. A well-designed logo will communicate confidence and professionalism. Use your logo consistently across all your marketing platforms.

Brand Photography

Personal branding photography is an important aspect of creating a strong brand. It involves capturing images that showcase your personality, style and professionalism. By investing in personal branding photography, you can differentiate yourself from your competitors and make a lasting impression on potential clients. Additionally, it's a great way to showcase you and your practice in a visually appealing way, which can help increase engagement and drive more traffic to your website. Personal branding photography can help you stand out from the crowd and capture the attention of your target audience.

A strong recommendation is to get a series of professional photographs taken. It's invaluable in conveying that personal image and appealing to your ideal clients. You'll use them throughout your marketing tools. The money you spend will not be wasted – promise! Expect to pay between £250 and £1500 for a half-day shoot. Choose the photographer carefully and look for one that has a portfolio showing the style of image you'd like.

Conclusion

Creating a marketing strategy for your private practice is all about truly figuring out and understanding with depth who your potential clients are and helping them to decide if you are the right therapist for them. It begins with knowing their desires, their struggles and how your therapy can be the solution they're seeking. It's about communicating your value with such a clarity and conviction that it not only reaches their ears but also resonates with their hearts, setting in motion a steady flow of client referrals. When you manage to bring all these pieces together, it will be a success!

Let's flip the script on traditional marketing. We're in the health and care business, and our marketing will be about guiding those in need to make choices that genuinely nurture their mental health. We're not about the hard sell; we're here to serve, empower and uplift those seeking support. Our marketing should be a clear, kind voice in a noisy, confusing world.

Your marketing strategy? It's your storytelling canvas. Being specific about who you help and how you help them makes all the difference. It's where understanding your audience makes content creation not just easy but enjoyable. It's where inclusivity is a genuine reflection of your practice's embrace.

Marketing takes time to build with consistency and quality. It's like a fine wine and matures with time. As for branding, Fiona Humberstone says it perfectly: 'Your brand should articulate the very essence of what makes you unique, weaving together your core values, your personality, and your style' (Humberstone, 2017). That's the brand that doesn't just get noticed; it gets remembered.

Let's think about more than just our marketing strategy as a way to fill our diaries. Think of it as your practice's pulse; the rhythm people will move to, trust and rely on. Your brand, your message, your consistency in delivering value – this is where the magic happens. It's not an overnight success; it's a journey. But it's one where every step counts, every client matters and every piece of content you create is a chapter in your practice's success story. Stick with it. The payoff is a practice that not only succeeds but also sincerely supports and transforms lives.

Business Plan Actions

Consider your marketing strategy and brand identity and work through the questions outlined in Figures 5.2 and 5.3.

BUSINESS PLANNING ACTION

EXPECT YOUR BRAND IDENTITY TO INCLUDE SOME OR ALL OF THE FOLLOWING:

- A DISTINCTIVE LOGO THAT'S INSTANTLY RECOGNISABLE ☐
- A COLOUR PALETTE THAT SUPPORTS YOUR BRAND VALUES ☐
- A RANGE OF TYPEFACES TO ADD CHARACTER ☐
- ILLUSTRATIONS TO ADD INTEREST AND PERSONALITY ☐
- PHOTOGRAPHY TO ADD CONSISTENCY AND DEPTH ☐
- PATTERNS AND DEVICES TO ADD TEXTURE AND FLAIR ☐

Image 5.2 Marketing your practice 1: A list of elements that make up a brand identity such as colour, logos and fonts.

BUSINESS PLANNING ACTION

ASK YOURSELF:

- WHAT IMPRESSION DO MY CURRENT WEBSITE AND MARKETING MATERIALS GIVE ABOUT MY BUSINESS?
- ARE THEY CONSISTENT?
- DO THEY REFLECT WHAT I WANT TO BE KNOWN FOR?
- AM I WINNING BUSINESS BECAUSE OF, OR IN SPITE OF, MY CURRENT BRAND IDENTITY?
- DO I FIND IT DIFFICULT TO GET MY CLIENTS TO SEE THE VALUE IN WHAT I'M DOING?
- AM I PROUD OF MY WEBSITE, BUSINESS CARD, LOGO AND MARKETING LITERATURE?

Figure 5.3 Marketing your practice 2: Questions to ask yourself about your current brand.

Chapter 6

Creating a Website

Sophie A. Wood

Introduction

The centrepiece of all your marketing activities is your website. It's your shop front – the place where potential clients will peer through the window and decide whether they would like to step inside and take a closer look. As with any shop, the owner's primary purpose is to encourage you to go through the door, take a browse, like what you see and hopefully make a purchase. A therapist's website is no different. You want visitors to arrive at your site, like what they see and get in touch. Its sole purpose is to encourage people to contact you. It's as simple as that.

The goal, therefore, is to build and design a website that achieves this. The primary foundation is to know who you are building your website for. Based on the work we've done in previous chapters, you'll have a clear image of your ideal client and the look and feel that will engage them.

The next step is to pull it all together and bring your website to life with the right design, content and functionality. Let's begin.

Why Is Your Website Important?

Websites are essential for businesses to establish credibility and build trust with your clients. When people are looking for a therapist, it's still high up there as one of the key methods people will use as part of their search.

On a website, potential clients can connect with your online presence and get to know you, which can have a massive impact on the success of your private practice, your ability to attract clients and how much money you make.

An effective website is important for several reasons:

1. *Credibility:* Having a professional website can help establish credibility for your business. In today's digital age, a website is often the first point of contact between a business and potential customers.
2. *Reach:* A website can help you reach a wider audience, both locally and globally, 24 hours a day, seven days a week.
3. *Cost-effectiveness:* Compared to traditional forms of advertising, a website is a cost-effective way to reach many people.

DOI: 10.4324/9781003401391-7

4. *Increased accessibility:* A website makes it easy for clients to find information about your products or services, contact information and business hours.
5. *Improved service:* A website can provide clients with access to information, advice and resources, improving client satisfaction and loyalty.
6. *Data collection and analysis:* A website can collect valuable data about your client and their behaviour, which can help inform your business decisions and improve your marketing strategies.

Overall, having a website for your business can help you establish and maintain a strong online presence, reach new clients and ultimately drive growth and success for your private practice.

Own Your Domain Name

A domain name is a unique name that identifies a website. It's the equivalent of your home address being where you live. The domain is where your website lives online, and it helps users find and access your website. For example, amazon.com and amazon.co.uk are the domain names for Amazon. It's not case sensitive, so don't worry about this side of things.

As it's part of your business identity and branding, it is best to own your own domain name. It needn't be the same as your business name, but people do tend to keep them aligned.

Tips for Choosing a Domain Name

- *Is it taken?* Check if the domain name is available for your website – 34SP allows you to check if a name is available from their home page (www.34sp. com). Also, check that the name is available for use on Facebook, X (formerly Twitter) or other social media platforms you might use.
- *Is it simple?* Try to keep a domain name simple and easy to spell so it's memorable.
- *Is it easy to say out loud?* Ensure your domain name can't be mistaken for anything else when said aloud. It needs clarity.
- *Do you like it?* You'll be saying it a lot, so best to like it!
- *Does it make sense for your business?* Your business name and domain name are part of your overall brand, so make sure they reflect this.

You can purchase domain names from many different places, and prices may vary. As the cost is relatively low per year (£10–£20), I would avoid the cheapest and go with the most reputable company with good security, such as Google Domains, GoDaddy and NameCheap. If available, purchase both. com and. co.uk.

Right, now we've got the domain name for your website so clients can find it. Before it goes live, you can ask your website developer to put up a 'coming soon' page. This will begin to build authority for your website so that when it goes live, you're not starting from scratch in terms of how familiar search engines are with your website. You could also ask people if they would like to provide you with their email address so you can let them know when your website is up and running. When your website is ready to go live, you'll use your domain name to point to where your new website is stored or hosted on the internet.

The Importance of Professional Photographs

A key element of a website that's often overlooked is photography. I'd strongly recommend investing in a series of professional photographs. You'll find they're invaluable for conveying that personal image and appealing to your ideal clients. As well as illustrating your website, you'll use them throughout your marketing. The money you spend will not be wasted – promise! Choose the photographer carefully and look for one that has a portfolio showing the style of image you'd like.

Spend a little time preparing for the shoot. Think about the clothes you'll wear, any props you'd like to use and even possible photographic settings. Your photographer should be able to help. It's also worth discussing the look and feel you're after. You could even create a mood board together. You want to get the most out of the shoot, so a little prep goes a long way. Also, the photographs needn't be all you. Images of your therapy room, its location, books, tools you use like your laptop and writing pads will all be useful too.

The photographs should convey who you are and how you want clients to feel when seeing you for therapy. Think safe, welcoming and professional.

Your Website Needs Content

For each page of your website, you'll need content in the form of written text and images. The content should be engaging, informative and relevant to your target audience.

A web designer may help with images and writing, but this is unusual. They will likely provide recommendations for content writers to go to. If you haven't the time or don't feel it's a skill in your wheelhouse, reach out to a content writer. Good content writers aren't cheap and are usually busy, so give yourself time to source the right one for you who can write in your voice and be authentic.

These are the core pages you'll need for your website and the key content you should have for each.

1. Home Page:

- Welcome intro to the website
- What you can help with
- Navigation menu or links to other important sections/pages
- Featured content or highlights

2. About Us/About Me Page:

   - Information about you
   - Background, history or achievements
   - Team members or key individuals
   - Contact information or links to contact details

3. Products/Services Page (recommend a page per modality used):

   - Description of the products or services offered
   - Product/service features and benefits

4. Testimonials/Reviews Page:

   - Collection of testimonials or reviews from satisfied customers or clients
   - Customer feedback on the products, services or overall experience

5. Blog/Articles Page:

   - List of blog posts or articles
   - Headlines and brief summaries of each blog post/article
   - Categories or tags for easy navigation
   - The comment section for readers to engage

6. Contact Page:

   - Contact information (such as address, phone number and email)
   - Contact form for visitors to send enquiries or messages
   - Social media links for additional contact options
   - Business hours or availability information

7. FAQ (Frequently Asked Questions) Page:

   - Common questions and answers related to the products or services
   - Clear and concise explanations for each question
   - Organised into categories for easy navigation

8. Privacy Policy:

   - Detailed information on how user data is collected, stored and used
   - Data protection measures and security practices
   - Cookie policy and opt-out options
   - Compliance with relevant laws and regulations

Website Design

The next step is to think about and plan the website's design. This includes the website's layout, colour choices, typography, and overall look and feel. Keeping the design consistent and user-friendly is essential so potential clients can easily navigate and understand the website. This should be aligned with the branding work we completed earlier.

While your website designer will ultimately help in this space, it's always best to go with your own thoughts and instincts about what you do and don't want. A few questions to ask yourself:

- How do you want people to feel when they interact with your brand? Safe and secure, edgy and excited, exclusive and cool, like they belong?
- Are there any particular colours you like for the website or colours you would like to avoid?
- Are there any other websites you particularly like the design of? Why?

Good Design and Great Functionality

Good design is about so much more than simply looking pretty. Just because a website looks nice doesn't mean it works well and will be instantly successful. Sometimes it can mean the opposite, especially if the most important element has been forgotten – your clients. Although the look and feel of your website's design is important, it also needs to be functional and easy to use.

Optimising your website so it works correctly on mobile devices is vital. This is known as making a website 'responsive.' This means the website responds to the screen sizes of different devices, automatically resizing content. Around half of the average small business website visitors use a smartphone or mobile device. For therapy practices, this can be even higher. A website that hasn't been optimised for mobile devices will deliver a poor experience. The key thing is, visitors aren't going to stay on your website if it's hard to use. Keep this in your mind as your website is being created.

Optimising Your Website to Be Found by Search Engines

Along with great design and functionality, optimising your website content to be found and understood by search engines so it will be shown in search results for your potential clients is critical to a successful website. This is known as search engine optimisation or SEO, which means maximising your website's content and structure to rank higher in search engine results, and in turn be shown to more of your ideal clients. In other words, we're talking about improving the visibility of your website and your business.

Your website designer should assist in this area as well. For the website as a whole, it needs to be fast loading. Preferably, when a user clicks on your website, it should load (i.e. become visible) in under 3 seconds. Google Page Speed Insights is one way to check the speed of a website.

As mentioned previously, your website also needs to work and be usable across mobile and tablet devices. Check if this is the case, or ask your web designer to confirm it is or will be once the website is launched.

You should also add your location to each page of the website, usually in the footer. It doesn't have to be a full address if this isn't possible; just a location would be enough for search engines to understand the geographic area you serve. This doesn't prevent you from ranking elsewhere geographically, but for a smaller business, it's important to rank somewhere location-wise.

Understanding Keywords

By keywords, we mean words or phrases that are closely aligned with searches you expect your ideal clients to make. When you use keywords in your website content and in the descriptions of images and the pages on your website, they help search engines such as Google understand the content. It also makes it easier for people to find relevant information when they search online. Think of keywords as the important words that capture the essence of what you're talking about. For example, if you're writing an article about dogs, some keywords might include 'dogs,' 'pets,' 'breeds,' or 'training.' These keywords give a clear idea of the main subject of your content.

When people search for something on the internet, they often type in keywords to find what they're looking for. Search engines like Google use these keywords to match them with relevant webpages and show the most helpful results. Choosing the right keywords is important because it helps your content be more discoverable and reach the right audience. By including keywords that accurately reflect your content's main ideas, you can increase its visibility and make it easier for people to find and benefit from your information and services.

You can identify these keywords through simple keyword research. This involves identifying specific terms or phrases used when searching for information related to your therapy service or business. You can use various tools and techniques, including Google AdWords Keyword Planner, Google Trends, and SEMrush. These tools provide valuable insights into keyword volume, competition and relevance, which tells you how many people used that search term in a given month, how many other businesses are trying to rank for this keyword and how relevant it is for your particular business/niche.

Let's look at a few examples of keywords that might be appropriate for therapist's websites:

- Help with Low Self-Esteem
- Therapy for Anxiety
- CBT Therapy for Anxiety
- CBT Therapist London
- EMDR Therapist
- Stress Symptoms
- Management of Anxiety

From this list, you can see how this works. You have to put yourself in the mind of the client and think about what keywords they would use. Then use the keyword research tools described here to explore these further.

Once you've done this research, the next step is to note what keyword(s) you want each page of your website to rank for. For example, a CBT therapist based in Bristol would likely want their home page to rank for 'CBT Therapist Bristol.' Then, when the website is being built, as they write the content, they will use these keyword terms both in the main text content of the page and in key headings, but also in the meta title (the title of a webpage), meta description and image ALT text (a descriptive text that is assigned to an image on a webpage). Your website designer should be able to advise on this as well. Still, it's worth having a grasp of the basics yourself. A website that isn't optimised for search engines is just a pretty website, nothing more.

Outside of speed, responsiveness and location, there are tasks to be done on each page of your website to help it rank with the search engines:

• Adding relevant keywords to the website's main headings. These are text elements that are used to organise and structure the content of a webpage. They are typically displayed in larger or bolder font than other text on the page. Headings are important for SEO, as they help to identify the most important content on the page. There are six levels of headings when creating website pages, ranging from H1 (the most important) to H6 (the least important). For SEO purposes, you need one H1 heading and two to three H2 headings only. These should reference your keywords.
• Adding relevant keywords to the website's body content.
• Optimising meta title tags and meta descriptions with keywords. A meta title is a webpage element that specifies the title of a webpage as it appears in search engine results and the browser's tab. A meta description is a webpage element that provides a brief description of the content of a webpage as it appears in search engine results. It should be designed to entice users to click through to the page.
• Adding an ALT tag to the images on your site. Short for 'alternative text,' an ALT tag is a description of an image included in a webpage's code. The purpose of ALT text is to provide a text alternative for people who are visually impaired and using screen readers to access the web, or when the image fails to load. It also has SEO value.

Building Your Website

We're well on our way now! We have a domain name, photographs, content and thoughts about the site's design, and we know the keywords we want the website to rank for. The next step is the build of the website. You can either do this yourself or have one done for you by a web design company. Your path will largely depend on what you want to achieve, how much time you've got and your budget. Remember, your website is an investment, not a cost. If done correctly, your website should more than pay for itself in the first year of operation.

You will likely want to link an email to your website. This involves creating a clickable link on a webpage that, when clicked, opens the user's default email client with a new message pre-populated with the designated email address. This functionality allows website visitors to contact you quickly, facilitates seamless communication and provides a convenient way for potential clients to reach out for enquiries.

If you have values around sustainability in your private practice, consider creating an eco-friendly website, which involves implementing sustainable practices throughout development and hosting. Choose a green web host, optimise code and file sizes, use responsive design and promote sustainability by minimising energy consumption and reducing carbon footprint.

Tips for a Successful Website Build

- Avoid using a friend/family member to build a website for you. Your website is a business tool and your primary method for attracting customers. You don't want to be running it on favours.
- When signing up for a website service, check what they need from you to start working on the website. You should expect to be asked at least basic questions about your business, the goals for the website, competitors, what websites you like and don't like, what functions you need on the website, provision of content (text and images) and SEO.
- When signing up for a website service, ask to see previous websites they have built in a similar business area to yours. Also, check out their testimonials.
- Check what the review process is going to be during the build so you can provide feedback. You should also ask what the process is if you wish to move suppliers at any point.
- Look for a website solution that will allow you to make small changes yourself but also offers support for larger changes.
- Ensure the website is going to be kept up to date on a monthly basis with software and security updates (to mitigate any risk of your website being hacked). This could also be a GDPR breach if you are taking client information through a content form.
- Ensure the website has some form of reporting available so you can see month-on-month the visitors you are getting and what they are doing on your website.

If you choose to work with a website designer, it will be a long-term relationship, so talk to a few before you decide who to work with. Is their process straightforward? If your website goes down, will they be responsive? It's technology – things do go wrong! Most importantly, knowing how to exit the relationship with a website designer is important for a smooth transition and to protect your interests and your private practice. Your business is constantly evolving, and it might be that after a few years you want to work with someone with a different approach. Clear communication and proper documentation are key. At the start, ask: if you need to move your website to another service, can you transfer it? Would you be able to have access to all website files, login credentials and domain information? Keep copies of all relevant communications and agreements for reference. By ending the relationship professionally and responsibly, you can smoothly transition to a new phase in managing your website.

How Much Should I Invest?

A good way to determine how much you should spend on your website is to figure out how much income you need it to generate. Imagine it's your shop front again. Do you want to be on the high street, or can your business survive on a side street where it's cheaper and there's less traffic?

Starting small is OK, especially if you're running your private practice part-time; your website won't need to work as hard. The DIY approach is not recommended unless you're reasonably tech-savvy and have plenty of time. You may not need an expensive bespoke website when you're just starting out, but you need something that works well and looks good. Prices vary significantly, from a relatively small set-up fee of £650 to bespoke designs of £2500 and upwards.

You'll also need to budget for ongoing maintenance of the site. A monthly expenditure will be needed to maintain the website – to keep your shop front secure and free from damage and keep the display fresh and appealing to potential clients. Budget around £30–£50 per month for this.

Which Platform Should I Use?

Many website builders are out there, from do-it-yourself solutions like Wix and Squarespace to more complex website solutions like WordPress and bespoke website builds. Each has its price point and pros and cons. Let's run through a few.

WordPress

Arguably the most popular website builder and blogging platform out there, Word-Press is behind an impressive number of pages on the internet, powering over 40% of the web! This is the platform I use when a client needs a bespoke website for their therapy practice.

Feel: professional, secure, customisable, high-ranking, versatile, scalable and user-friendly.

Pros

- WordPress gives you complete control over your website, and you can structure the content to your needs.
- The vast collection of WordPress plugins allows you to create the necessary functionality.
- WordPress websites have a good chance of ranking higher than others. With its SEO-friendly themes and dedicated SEO tools, you can increase your visibility and reach more potential clients.
- As a healthcare practitioner, you deal with important patient data that needs to be accessed easily. WordPress stores data efficiently and lets you download it anytime with just one click.
- As your practice grows, your website needs to grow too. Platforms powered by WordPress scale well, and you can easily keep adding content and features.

Cons

- Even though the WordPress dashboard is meant to be user-friendly, some users find it takes time to master. There can be a steep learning curve, especially for those who are not familiar with website building or coding, so it may take time to master the platform.
- Requires regular updates. WordPress, its themes and plugins require frequent updates to maintain security and functionality. If updates are not made regularly, it can put your website at risk of security breaches or compatibility issues.
- With WordPress, you are responsible for your hosting needs. However, installing WordPress on hosting platforms like Bluehost or Dreamhost is an easy process that should only take a few minutes.

Costs

WordPress is free and open-source. You will need to purchase hosting, which can start from £4 to £6 per month. Free and paid themes and plugins are available. Bespoke design costs vary depending on your specific needs but range from £500 to £3000.

Overall, WordPress is a highly customisable, scalable and flexible platform that is ideal for therapy businesses of all sizes and is a good choice for those who want more control over the design and functionality of their website.

Pocket Site

Pocket Site is one of the only website builders that is specifically designed for therapists and mental health professionals. There are several benefits to using Pocket Site for building a website; it provides professionally developed templates tailored to the mental health field, saving time and effort. It has a user-friendly interface and drag-and-drop functionality. Customisation is easy. Integrated appointment scheduling, secure client portals and HIPAA-compliant forms enhance the therapeutic experience.

Feel: personal, bespoke, user-friendly, health care centred and secure.

Pros

- It's easy to customise every aspect of the website. You can select a pre-built template, and there's a starter site included as standard.
- Easy to use. Pocket Site is user-friendly and requires no coding or design skills to create a professional-looking website.
- Customisable templates. Pocket Site offers a range of customisable templates to help you create a website that accurately reflects your brand and services.
- Secure. Security is a top priority for Pocket Site, and all websites created with the platform are kept secure. This means that patient data is protected and kept confidential.

- Built-in SEO. Pocket Site includes built-in SEO features as standard, helping your website to rank higher in search engine results and making it easier for potential clients to find you online.
- Affordable pricing. Pocket Site offers affordable pricing options, making it accessible for therapists and mental health professionals of all budgets.
- Pocket Site has a built-in image library.
- GDPR is ready to go with a privacy and cookie policy built in.
- There's no need to worry about keeping your site up to date, safe and secure, as it's all done for you.
- Step-by-step training videos to get you going quickly and personalised support.

Cons

- More costly per month than most, but this includes excellent support and your site is hosted on one of the fastest, most secure and most reliable hosting environments around – WP Engine.
- You need to spend time on the platform to get the most out of the platform, so it's not for everyone.

Costs

There's no set-up charge unless you are looking for Pocket Site to design your website for you, which costs £600–£700; then, your Pocket Site fee is just a flat £30–£40 per month at the time of writing. There's no contract, and you can terminate at any time. You can have a 30-minute free consultation before committing to ensure it's the right platform for you. And a design service is also available if you need a helping hand to get going.

In summary, Pocket Site offers a user-friendly, customisable, secure and affordable solution for therapists looking to build a professional website.

Wix

With drag-and-drop customisation and a dedicated customer support team, Wix has gained popularity as a great website builder for beginners.

Feel: friendly interface, easy, customisable, user-friendly and suitable for beginners.

Pros

- Joining the Wix platform and getting started is simple and easy from the start.
- After choosing your theme, the Wix editor gives you total freedom. You can drag and drop sections of text and media. You can resize, align and reorder them quickly. There are also multiple Wix plugins to choose from to add new features to your platform.

- The Wix editor shows you how your website looks on different devices and lets you customise PC, mobile and tablet versions. You can also realign and customise different elements to fit smaller screens.
- Due to its clean structure and ease, the Wix website builder is great for portfolios and personal pages.

Cons

- Total freedom sounds great, but the website might have poor visuals if you aren't inclined towards web design or are short on time.
- Wix websites don't scale well and, depending on the amount of content and features you add, the pages will load slower.
- You cannot change it once you choose a theme and publish your therapy website. This means any future rebrand or redesign must be done within the limits of the respective theme.
- There's no personalised support.
- Performance issues. Depending on the size and complexity of your website, you may experience slow loading times or other performance issues, which can negatively impact the user experience.
- If you build your website on Wix, you will be dependent on the Wix platform and limited in terms of what you can do with your website outside of the Wix ecosystem.
- Even though they offer their own SEO tools, websites published with Wix seem harder to optimise. Wix has limited SEO capabilities, making it difficult for your website to rank well in search engine results.

Costs

Wix has a free plan available that you can use to try out the platform, along with multiple premium plans. The lower-price tiers are perfect for a personal or portfolio website, but for a professional business website, you will need a business or eCommerce plan that starts from £15/month. Overall, Wix is a flexible and affordable website builder with a wide range of features and capabilities, making it a good choice for a starter business needing an online presence.

Squarespace

Known for various great-looking themes, designers and creative professionals often use Squarespace to build visually appealing websites.

Feel: creative, professional, ready-made, good-looking, secure, standardised.

Pros

- A Squarespace website builder is known for its creative themes and beautiful layouts.

- With Squarespace, you get everything you need by choosing the right template for your website. The Squarespace features are integrated with their layouts, which makes it friendly for beginners or people who don't want to spend much time on design.
- Squarespace offers features specifically designed for eCommerce so the user can add subscription pages, shopping carts, or catalogue sections. It also provides scheduling tools for booking appointments.
- Squarespace has an excellent customer service team, and since they keep everything in-house, they will handle any issues or enquiries.

Cons

- Since Squarespace works with templates, there is only so much you can customise when it comes to design. Squarespace websites can look alike, which means you might lose brand recognition.
- When it comes to SEO, Squarespace can be difficult to optimise. The templates do not perform as well as other websites, their internal SEO tools can be hard to learn and it doesn't allow for third-party plugins that could help with a higher ranking.
- Even though they offer a great selection of possibilities, the features you can add to a Squarespace website are limited.
- Since Squarespace works with predetermined templates, it can be challenging to expand your website.

Costs

Squarespace offers four pricing options. For a personal plan, the price starts at £24/month when paid annually (or £17 on a monthly basis), and it goes up to £30/month annually for an advanced eCommerce platform at the time of writing.

If you contact a website designer, they are likely using one of these four platforms to build your site using their expertise with that particular platform. This saves you the learning curve and will provide a quicker and more likely better solution than doing it yourself. Some designers will code a website from scratch, but it's best to avoid this type of solution as it becomes problematic to support should the web designer go out of business or the relationship break down. More than likely, you'll be left having to rebuild the site again from scratch and pay the resulting costs for this. These types of designs are becoming less common as website builder tools become better and better.

Your Website Is Built – What Now?

Once your website is built, you should have already had a couple of opportunities to review the website prior to completion and provide feedback. Now, you can do final testing for usability and functionality before it goes live. Complete the following:

- Check for broken links across the site.
- Ensure that contact forms work.
- Ensure any reporting/analytics is set up and accessible by you.
- Check that buttons and navigation are all working.
- Is your location on each page?
- Ensure clear and sufficient calls to action (i.e. contact me) are on all pages.
- Check that there is good linking from one page of the site to another so no page is an orphan – left with no links to other pages.
- Check that the website works across different devices – desktop, mobile and tablet. Mobile is the most important.
- Is the website speed OK?
- Is the text all readable and not too small, especially on mobile?
- Check that your keywords are present on each page.
- Check that the meta title and meta descriptions are in place.
- Check that styling is all aligned with your selected branding.
- Check the alignment for text and images – everything aligned to something, nothing visually disturbing.
- Check that no more than two typefaces are used and there are consistent type-face sizes for headings and buttons.
- Ensure that the website is being backed up.
- Ensure all passwords are strong and secure.
- Ensure any placeholder images or text are removed or replaced.
- Check privacy and cookie policies are in place.

Post Website Launch Activities – Looking After Your Website

Now that your website is live, it's important to remember that to attract traffic (potential clients), it needs to be attractive to Google and, in turn, your customers. You can do this by offering fresh, new or updated content regularly, in the form of blogs, educational videos or downloads and by ensuring you advertise it on your social media profiles.

Setting up a schedule for publishing content is worthwhile. Consistency is important. Posting every Wednesday is far better than posting one week on Tuesday and another week on Friday; you'll get more Google love with consistency. Remember to post links to the new content across all social media platforms. In the case of X and Facebook, you may re-post content several times a day due to the speed of the news feeds – it's easy for content to be missed.

By far the hardest, but one of the most important things to do is to get other websites pointing to your website via backlinks. Backlinks are links that direct users from other websites to your own. When reputable websites link to your site, particularly those that Google recognises as authoritative, it significantly boosts your website's credibility and visibility in search engine rankings. For example, if a well-known mental health organisation like Anxiety UK links to your therapy practice website as a reliable resource, it adds significant weight to your website's authority. This can result in higher visibility and improved rankings in search engine results, ultimately driving more traffic to your website.

Finally, create a buzz around the launch of your website. Email your existing contact database to inform them about the launch of your website. Post about it on social media and add the link to all your marketing materials, invoices, and email signatures.

Conclusion

Building a successful website requires careful consideration and implementation of various elements. It starts with understanding the importance of headings for search engine optimisation and utilising relevant keywords throughout the website's content. By structuring the content effectively and incorporating targeted keywords, therapy businesses can improve their website's visibility and attract more potential clients.

When it comes to the website build itself, there are different platforms to choose from with pros and cons for each. However, regardless of the platform chosen, investing in a well-designed and functional website is essential. While starting small is acceptable, it is important to align the investment with the income-generation goals of the business. Ongoing maintenance and budgeting for updates are crucial to ensure that the website remains secure and up to date. Additionally, considering the platform's ability to scale, reporting capabilities and support for both small and large changes is essential for long-term success.

Throughout the website-building process, clear communication with website designers, reviewing previous work and understanding the review process are important factors to consider. Having reporting and analytics in place allows practitioners to monitor website performance and visitor behaviour, enabling them to make informed decisions to improve their online presence.

Once the website is live, conducting thorough testing is crucial to ensure its usability and functionality. This includes checking for broken links, testing contact forms and ensuring compatibility across different devices. Ongoing activities such as creating fresh and engaging content, promoting the website on social media and seeking backlinks from reputable sources contribute to its visibility and credibility.

By considering these key points and taking strategic actions, therapy businesses can attract potential clients, enhance their credibility and support their overall growth and success. Remember, your website is an investment, not a cost. Its creation will probably require time, effort and money, but you'll earn these things back quickly if you do it right.

Business Plan Actions

Figure 6.1 outlines the business planning actions for you to consider and complete in detail for this chapter. Take your time to carefully analyse each question and task, providing thoughtful and comprehensive responses. It is important to dedicate enough effort and attention to these questions and tasks, as they will serve as the foundation for your business plan. Remember, the more detailed and comprehensive your answers, the better prepared you will be to develop a successful and effective business plan for your website.

CREATING A WEBSITE - CHECKLIST

- ☐ DOMAIN NAME PURCHASED
- ☐ PROFESSIONAL PHOTOGRAPHS DONE
- ☐ WEBSITE CONTENT DRAFTED
- ☐ DOCUMENTED THOUGHTS AROUND THE LAYOUT, COLOUR, TYPOGRAPHY, AND LOOK AND FEEL FOR THE WEBSITE
- ☐ SEARCH ENGINE OPTIMISATION – KEYWORD RESEARCH COMPLETED
- ☐ CLEAR BUDGET IN MIND FOR BOTH SETUP AND ONGOING SUPPORT FOR THE WEBSITE
- ☐ RESEARCHED AND SELECTED A WEB DESIGNER – CHECKED "TIPS FOR A WEBSITE"
- ☐ REGULAR CHECKPOINTS IN PLACE TO REVIEW THE DATA YOU HOLD AND YOUR PROCESSES
- ☐ COMPLETED FINAL CHECKS ON THE WEBSITE
- ☐ ONGOING MAINTENANCE, SUPPORT AND ANALYTICS IN PLACE
- ☐ SCHEDULE FOR PUBLISHING CONTENT TO THE WEBSITE REGULARLY
- ☐ WORK ONGOING TO GET OTHER WEBSITES TO POINT TO YOUR WEBSITE

Figure 6.1 Creating a website: A checklist of things to consider.

Chapter 7

Data Protection

Sophie A. Wood

Introduction

Data protection is the measures you take to safeguard personal and sensitive information from unauthorised access, use, disclosure or destruction. It can include technical security measures, policies and procedures designed to protect sensitive information from cyber threats, data breaches (when sensitive or confidential information is accessed, stolen or used without authorisation) or accidental loss. For therapists, this means protecting client data – personal information and sensitive information held with client notes. This chapter will help you feel confident in your ability to manage data protection in your practice effectively.

Data protection regulations vary by country, so it is important to research and understand your region's specific laws and guidelines. It is also essential to regularly review and update your data protection policies and procedures to ensure compliance with any new regulations or changes. First and foremost, as a therapist, it is crucial to maintain the confidentiality and privacy of your client's data and to communicate clearly with them about how their data is being used and protected.

Data protection is of particular concern for therapists, especially in light of recent developments like GDPR in the UK and Europe. Globally, there is a growing emphasis on protecting data from harm and illegal access and ensuring that the data owner (the client) understands how, why and where their data is being used, as well as the rights they have over it.

Data Protection Across the Globe

- Data protection laws in the UK (and Europe) are designed to protect individuals' personal data from being misused or mishandled. These laws regulate how personal data is collected, used, stored and shared by organisations. In the UK, the data protection law is called the Data Protection Act 2018, and it is the General Data Protection Regulation (GDPR) in Europe.
- If you hold personal data in the UK, you must also register with the Information Commissioner's Office (ICO), which enforces data protection laws. All therapists will need to do this.

DOI: 10.4324/9781003401391-8

- Data protection laws in Australia and New Zealand regulate the collection, use, disclosure and storage of personal information. These laws aim to protect individuals' privacy and ensure organisations are not misused or mishandled. In both Australia and New Zealand, these issues fall under what is known as the Privacy Act.
- Data protection in the United States refers to the laws and regulations that protect individuals' personal information from unauthorised access, use or disclosure by organisations. Several US laws protect data, including the Health Insurance Portability and Accountability Act (HIPAA) and the California Consumer Privacy Act (CCPA).
- Data protection in Canada refers to the Personal Information Protection and Electronic Documents Act (PIPEDA), which sets out rules for how private sector organisations collect, use and disclose personal information during commercial activities.

While it is very easy to become overloaded with the rules and regulations of data protection, it's important not to overthink it and keep in mind the basic point of all data protection legislation with regards to therapists: you need to make sure your clients' data and privacy is secure and protected at all times.

Key Points to Remember

- Only collect data that is essential for the service you are performing.
- Delete the data when you or your client no longer needs it.
- Store all data responsibly.
- Ensure your client clearly understands the data you are collecting and why.
- Disclose the data to other parties only when legally obliged or consented to by your client.

These are the main points, and being able to evidence the preceding points in operation in your practice is all you need to do. You can evidence it by undertaking an annual data protection audit.

What Does This All Mean for You?

Now that we have established the importance of data protection for your practice, let's explore the steps you can take to keep on the right side of data protection. We'll take a practical step-by-step approach.

Understand What 'Data' You Hold

When you operate a therapy business, data comes in many forms. We often think of it as purely client personal details and session data, but we should not forget you also control/look after other data outside this. For example, financial data, email marketing data and website visitor data. As a first step, identify all the personal data you hold.

A Mini Audit:

- Names
- Physical addresses
- Email addresses
- Health data – mental or physical
- Behavioural data, collected by observing how people interact online
- Location data
- Financial information

For each element of data, ask yourself a few questions:

- Where is the data stored – paper, laptop, cloud, email or online private practice software for taking clinical notes?
- What is the data?
- When was the data collected?
- What type of data is it – personal, sensitive data? Personal data refers to any information that can be used to identify an individual. In contrast, sensitive data refers to information that is considered confidential or private, such as financial information or medical records.
- What business process does it support (client sessions, email marketing, recruitment, website visitor data, financial)?
- Why do you hold the data? Is it required for the delivery of therapy? Marketing or research purposes?
- What is the lawful basis for holding the data? (The lawful basis for a therapist to hold data pertains to compliance with UK and EU data protection laws. Therapists should verify the legal grounds for data processing and consult their local regulatory authorities for specific guidelines.) For purposes of a therapist, this falls into two areas:

  1. The legal basis likely falls under 'legitimate interests' for recording and storing client notes and related information. This is a flexible lawful basis that applies when you use a client's data in a way they would reasonably expect and with minimal privacy impact. When a client registers and attends treatment sessions with you, they expect you to keep a record of their contact details so you can contact them to arrange and discuss treatment and keep a record of your sessions with them to assist in their ongoing therapy.
  2. Notes of treatment sessions with clients are likely to fall under the definition of special category data, classed as sensitive data. You need an additional condition for using and storing this data. Processing is necessary for your role as a healthcare professional delivering healthcare services.

- Do I need to continue to hold this data?
- How long will the data be held (retention period)?
- Is the data accurate?
- Are there any third parties involved in the processing of the data?

As a responsible data owner, you should understand the data you hold, why and where. I recommended keeping a copy of this audit and running it each year. At pocketsite.co.uk, we offer a Compliance Pack to help with this audit process.

As part of this, you may identify data you no longer need to keep. If you don't need to keep it, then delete it. Many therapists hold client data for 7–8 years beyond the date therapy ends to comply with business insurance requirements. Contact your liability insurance company and check how long they require you to keep data for.

Data tends to be kept in case a client claims against you or your private practice. This is usually extended for children until they reach 25 years of age. If you're holding data beyond 7–8 years or beyond 25 years of age for a child you treated, double check if it's actually needed by your insurers or data protection regulations specific to the country your business is located in. Of course, if you have particular concerns about a client and could justify those concerns by retaining the data longer, then you should do so.

Protecting Your Business Data

Now you understand the data you hold and why and you have removed any unnecessary data that is no longer needed. Your next step is to look closely at how you store this data. Remember, one of the central tenets of data protection is to protect the data from unauthorised access or breach. Many laws say you must take 'appropriate security measures' without really saying what they actually expect. We need to read between the lines and make our best guess at what constitutes reasonable measures to take in storing data. Let's be clear – no one is expecting your small business to operate under the same security as the Bank of England or the Federal Reserve. It's about being appropriate.

The data you hold should only be accessible to you or your client and those authorised to do so (and those individuals should only use the data within the scope of the authority given to them). The data shouldn't be available for unauthorised access. The data should remain accessible and usable, i.e., if the data is lost, altered or destroyed, you can recover it to prevent any damage or distress to the client concerned.

You will more than likely have six essential methods for storing data covering:

- Paper-based
- Desktop/laptop/USB stick
- Cloud storage – Google Drive, DropBox, OneDrive
- Email
- Website
- Online practice management software and other Software as a Service (SaaS) solutions

When it comes to storing data securely and responsibly, there are several factors to consider depending on which method or combination of methods you use.

If you store data on paper, keeping it in a secure location, such as a locked filing cabinet and limiting access to only those who need it is essential. Additionally, it is advisable to use a system that tracks who has accessed the data, when and for what reason. It is also important to ensure the data is destroyed securely once it is no longer needed.

When storing data on a desktop, laptop or USB stick, it is crucial to use strong passwords, encryption and other security measures to protect against unauthorised access. This includes using password managers, for example OnePass, to generate and store strong passwords and keeping your operating system and software up to date with the latest security patches. Using a password manager is a great way to control and manage passwords. They also offer 'two-factor authentication' or 'two-step authentication' options using a password and physical security key (controlled by your fingerprint). Backing up the data regularly and storing the backups in a separate location is also a good practice in case of data loss or theft.

You can also purchase computer anti-theft cables that connect to your computer and then are secured at the other end on a desk or similar heavy object to prevent opportunistic theft of a device.

Cloud storage services like Google Drive, Dropbox or OneDrive offer convenient and easily accessible storage options that comply with international security standards, such as IS27001, a well-known standard for managing and protecting sensitive information. Check that other suppliers you use are compliant with this standard. You can also take extra precautions to ensure the security of your data. This includes using two-factor authentication and strong passwords as mentioned earlier.

Email Data Protection

Keeping your emails secure is a crucial aspect of data protection for all businesses, including private practices. Emails often contain personal and sensitive data, making them a prime target for cybercriminals and hackers. Therefore, it is essential to implement security measures to protect this information from unauthorised access and misuse.

One of the most effective ways to protect email data is through encryption. Encryption involves encoding the contents of an email in a way that can only be deciphered by the intended recipient. This ensures that even if an unauthorised person intercepts the email, they cannot read its contents.

Access controls/user permissions are another important aspect of email data protection. These ensure that only authorised personnel can access sensitive emails and their content. This can include requiring strong passwords, multi-factor authentication, and limiting access to certain individuals or groups.

Email data should be stored securely, with access restricted to authorised personnel. This means ensuring your laptop or desktop is kept secure using the methods mentioned previously. Your email service provider should also store the data securely. They must comply with international standards for security, such as IS27001. Providers should also offer options for two-factor authentication and strong passwords. For therapy practices, using robust and secure email services is very important. Using a paid email service such as Google's Workspace offering or Microsoft's 365 offering would be best practice. These services offer encryption when the data is transmitted (via a protocol called 'TLS,' or Transport Layer Security) and where it is stored. Both companies are compliant to ISO27001, GDPR and HIPAA standards and are regularly audited for compliance to these. For security reasons, these services would always be a preference for therapists over and above email services bundled in as part of your website hosting or domain purchase.

Website Data Protection

When it comes to your website, data protection best practice refers to the recommended methods and procedures for protecting personal information collected by websites. This can include measures such as secure data storage, encryption and policies for informing users about how their data is being used and protecting their privacy.

You should ensure the use of secure connections (HTTPS) on your website. HTTPS is a protocol that encrypts data between a user's web browser and the website, preventing unauthorised access to the data in transit. Most websites have this as standard today, but some legacy sites still operate without it. Check to see if your website uses HTTPS.

Another critical factor to consider is implementing strong password policies. Passwords are a common target for cybercriminals and hackers, and weak passwords can easily be guessed or cracked. Therefore, it is essential to ensure all users of your website (you, the website support person, the virtual assistant) use strong passwords that are difficult to guess and to implement policies such as password expiration and two-factor authentication to provide an additional layer of security.

It is also important to regularly update software to prevent vulnerabilities. Hackers often take advantage of vulnerabilities in outdated software to gain access to a website's data. Therefore, ensure your website is regularly updated with software to ensure that it remains secure and protected.

You should also ensure any SaaS you use is protecting your data adequately for data protection. These applications may include email, customer relationship management (CRM) or online practice management solutions. For the suppliers you use, ensure you have a strong password in place, possibly using two-factor authentication mentioned earlier in the chapter. Limit access to your account to only those essential individuals. Check that each supplier is compliant with recognised data protection standards such as ISO 27001, GDPR and HIPAA. It is your responsibility to ensure that wherever you store data, you have done the appropriate homework on that third party to ensure they will look after the data and process it in line with your wishes.

In all cases, it is important to regularly review and update the security measures you have in place to ensure they are up to date and effective. It is also important to have a plan in place in case of a security breach or data loss, including a process for notifying affected individuals and relevant authorities. By taking these steps, you can help to ensure that the data you store remains secure and protected.

Making Sure Your Client Understands the Data You're Collecting and Why

OK, so far you've completed an audit of the data you hold in your practice, reviewed how you store the data, ensured it's held securely and removed any data you no longer need. The next step is all about communicating clearly and concisely to your clients about the data you will hold about them and your client's acknowledgement of this.

Therapy Agreements

For many therapists, this is usually all wrapped up in one document, the therapy agreement or contract. Such a document may cover several aspects of how you deliver therapy and the client's obligations, but it can also act as a privacy notice.

Having one document seems more sensible than two separate ones when you're trying to onboard multiple clients. It can get confusing as to who has approved what. I'd advocate for simplicity and go with the one document.

A typical therapy agreement, including privacy notice/data protection elements, would have the following sections.

- *Introduction:* Provide an overview of the therapy agreement and why it is in place. Include a brief description of the therapy service being offered.
- *Professional conduct:* Outline the professional code of conduct you will adhere to during therapy sessions.
- *Therapy sessions length, cost and cancellation policy:* Outline how they can rearrange or cancel an appointment and where it will take place (i.e. online or in person).
- *Termination of service:* Outline a policy detailing the procedure for termination of the therapy service.
- *Personal information:* When you request personal information (such as any medication the client uses and their GP surgery details), the client has a right to know why this information is needed, under what circumstances it may be used and how it will be securely stored.
- *Record keeping:* Clients should understand that therapists may find it helpful to take notes during sessions. Explain that these tend to be brief and are designed to help them keep track of topics/themes covered in therapy. Highlight the fact notes are kept in a locked cabinet or in password-protected documents, on a secure platform or on practitioner computers per the data protection act and GDPR.
- *Confidentiality and privacy notice:* Write a statement on the confidentiality and privacy of the client's data. Explain that confidentiality will be maintained within the codes of ethics and legal requirements. You should also state when

confidentiality rules do not apply, for example, if you have concerns about your client's or others' safety.

- *Communication:* Outline your preferred communication methods (e.g. phone, email) and response times for non-emergency situations. Include any boundaries around communication outside of scheduled sessions.
- *Emergency procedures:* Provide instructions for clients to follow in case of a mental health crisis or emergency, including relevant contact information for crisis support services.
- *Details of supervision:* You should explain that therapists must have regular supervision sessions to discuss aspects of their clinical work. Emphasise that they do not reveal individual identities during these sessions and that supervision itself is confidential between therapist and supervisor.
- *How to make a complaint:* Give details of your complaints procedure and how these complaints will be handled – for example, how long you will endeavour to respond and your professional body details.

This list isn't prescriptive. You may want to include further sections depending on how you prefer to operate.

Let's focus a little more on the data-specific elements in the agreement and expand these further. There are no hard and fast rules here, merely what would be considered best practice and sensible to include to ensure your clients are fully aware of the data you will be holding on them. The agreement should:

- Include details of who you are and how to contact you.
- Explain your clients' rights over their information. For example:

You can access and obtain a copy of your data and correct inaccuracies. You also have the right to delete your data in certain situations, limit its use, and transfer it to another company. You can refuse the use of your data in certain ways and object to decisions made about you based on automated processing.

This last part may be applicable in any automated assessments you perform using client data – for example, automated autism assessments.
- Specify the personal and sensitive data you collect and how it is used.
- Explain how and why the information is collected during assessments to deliver therapy services.
- Provide details of who the information will be shared with and why, including that explicit consent will be requested if shared outside of the supervisor or other party mentioned.
- State how long the data will be held and that it will be securely destroyed.
- State that the information is held securely.
- State the lawful basis for using and holding the data. For personal details, it is based on the contract to deliver therapy. It can be based on sensitive data and will vary from country to country based on the conditions and safeguards

associated with a professionally recognised body the therapist is a member of, or the client's consent.

Remember, consent is required for sharing data with third parties outside of those explicitly mentioned in the agreement.

Using Your Therapy Agreement

The agreement sections mentioned in the previous section are meant to cover a typical therapist scenario. You should modify them based on your own needs. Once you've customised the agreement, you can start using it with your clients. It's important for clients to read and understand the agreement and privacy information. You may need to spend some time explaining it to them. This will reassure you that the client understands you will be holding sensitive information on them and for how long. It also presents you as a professional therapist who takes responsibility for the privacy of client data seriously.

Getting the client to sign the form as proof they have read and understood it is useful. You may photocopy one original or ask the client to sign two documents. Whichever method you use, you need to retain clear evidence of their consent along with your session notes according to your data retention policy.

A physical signature may be impossible if you're working with clients online. In this case, you could ask the client to print out the form, sign it and send you a photograph of the signed form or an email confirming their consent. You should keep this confirmation with the session notes.

The therapy agreement should be written in simple language so it can be easily understood. If you're providing therapy services to children, you'll need parental consent for those under a certain age. This varies from country to country, so you should check the rules where you are.

Other Data Protection/Privacy Notices

We've been discussing the therapy agreement in this chapter, but we shouldn't overlook other areas of your practice that will need a privacy notice to be available.

If you have a website or use email marketing services, you must provide clear privacy notices explaining what data you collect, why you collect it, how it is stored, who it is shared with and how long it will be held.

Your privacy notices should also explain how clients can exercise their rights over their data, such as accessing, correcting, or deleting their data. This information will help to build trust with your clients and demonstrate that you take their privacy seriously.

When it comes to email marketing, it's important to ensure clients have given explicit consent to receive marketing emails from you. You should provide a transparent opt-in process for clients to subscribe to your emails and an easy-to-use opt-out process. Additionally, you should only send marketing emails to clients who have consented, and include an easy way for them to unsubscribe from future emails.

It is important to keep privacy notices up to date and comply with any new regulations or changes. This can be daunting, but it is crucial to review and update your privacy notices regularly to ensure that they remain relevant and accurate.

By providing clear and concise privacy notices on your website and email marketing materials, you can build trust with your clients and demonstrate that you take data protection seriously. This, in turn, can help to improve your business reputation and increase client loyalty.

Third Parties – Processing Client Data

From time to time, therapists may engage with other companies or individuals to help in their business, for example accountants, virtual assistants, solicitors and marketing specialists. It's crucial for data protection that any parties connected to your business with access to personal and sensitive data have a specific agreement in place for how they will access, use and store data. Your responsibility as the owner of the client data is to ensure that you have vetted carefully and agreed on how any third parties may use the data and have an agreement in place with them around this. At Pocket Site, we provide a Data Processing Agreement for therapists to help here.

The following are key sections that could be included in a data processing agreement scenario:

1. *Introduction:* An overview of what the agreement entails and the parties involved.
2. *Definitions:* Definitions of key terms used in the agreement.
3. *Scope of services:* A description of the services to be provided by the data processor.
4. *Responsibilities:* A statement of the responsibilities of each party.
5. *Data Protection:* A description of the measures taken to protect the data.
6. *Data processing:* A description of the data processing activities to be performed by the data processor. How the data will be manipulated/used – data entry, validation, sorting, analysis and reporting.
7. *Data security:* A description of the security measures taken to protect the data.
8. *Data subject rights:* A description of the data subject rights and how they will be handled.
9. *Sub-processors:* – A statement on sub-processors' use and any restrictions on their use.
10. *Data breaches:* – A description of the data breach notification process.
11. *Data protection impact assessment:* – A statement on the data protection impact assessment process and how it will be performed.
12. *Term and termination:* A statement on the term and termination of the agreement.
13. *Governing law:* A statement on the agreement's governing law.
14. *Dispute Resolution:* A statement on the dispute resolution process.

Remember, the specific sections and language used in a data processing agreement may vary depending on the parties involved and the nature of the data processing activities. For example, accountants may already have draft agreements available that you simply need to review and satisfy yourself that the data will be processed in line with the services requested of the third party and that the data is held securely. Don't forget to include details on how data will be removed once you exit an arrangement.

Conclusion

In today's world, data protection has become a crucial aspect for all businesses, and therapy practices are no exception. Ensuring data protection in your therapy practice is essential for the privacy and security of your clients' information. By following the guidelines and best practices outlined in this chapter, you can create a robust data protection framework that safeguards sensitive data from unauthorised access and potential breaches.

Remember to conduct regular audits of the data you hold, reviewing and removing any unnecessary information to minimise risk. Take appropriate security measures when storing data, whether it be in physical or digital form, and consider using encryption and strong passwords to protect against unauthorised access.

Communicating clearly with your clients about the data you collect and why is crucial to establish trust and transparency. Incorporating a comprehensive therapy agreement that includes privacy notices ensures that clients fully understand your data collection practices and their rights regarding their personal information.

Additionally, it is important to extend data protection measures to other areas of your practice, such as your website and email communications. Implement secure connections, encryption and strong password policies to safeguard client data.

Collaborating with third parties requires a specific data processing agreement that outlines how data will be accessed, used and stored by these parties. Vetting and selecting trustworthy partners is crucial to maintaining the integrity of your clients' data.

By prioritising data protection and adhering to legal and ethical obligations, you establish yourself as a professional who values client privacy and confidentiality. This commitment not only strengthens your reputation but also fosters client loyalty and trust.

Remember, data protection is an ongoing process. Stay updated with the latest regulations and best practices, regularly review and update your security measures and educate yourself on emerging threats. By doing so, you can continue to provide a safe and secure environment for your clients and their data.

Your dedication to data protection sets the foundation for a successful and ethical therapy practice. Let your commitment to privacy be a lasting impression that resonates with your clients, ensuring their trust and confidence in your services.

Build Your Business Plan

Consider and complete the business planning questions and tasks (provided in Figure 7.1) in detail to create a strong foundation for your business plan.

DATA PROTECTION CHECKLIST

- [ ] DATA AUDIT COMPLETE
- [ ] DATA STORED SECURELY / STRONG PASSWORDS
- [ ] THERAPY AGREEMENT – PRIVACY NOTICE SECTIONS WRITTEN
- [ ] CLIENT ONBOARDING PROCESS INCLUDES THERAPY AGREEMENT SIGN OFF
- [ ] PRIVACY NOTICE AVAILABLE ON WEBSITE AND EMAIL MARKETING COMMS
- [ ] AGREEMENTS IN PLACE WITH ANY 3RD PARTIES PROCESSING CLIENT DATA EG VIRTUAL ASSISTANTS
- [ ] FAMILIAR WITH DATA PROTECTION GUIDELINES IN YOUR COUNTRY
- [ ] REGULAR CHECKPOINTS IN PLACE TO REVIEW THE DATA YOU HOLD AND YOUR PROCESSES
- [ ] REGISTER WITH THE APPROPRIATE DATA PROTECTION AGENCY FOR YOUR COUNTRY (UK – THIS IS THE ICO)

Figure 7.1 Data protection checklist.

Chapter 8

Getting Ready for Therapy Sessions

Introduction

In private practice, the moments before a client walks through the door are as important as the session itself. You've done a lot of the groundwork in the previous chapters, and this chapter will get you ready for the moment your client walks in or logs onto their first therapy session with you; we'll explore the essential elements you need to have in place. We'll discuss how to establish a practical framework for your ideal working week and provide an overview of time management strategies to support your schedule and maintain the balance of therapists and business owners. Clarifying how to blend clinical excellence with the nuanced roles required in running a business, ensuring that you are equipped with all the necessary tools, all the paperwork you will need, organised diaries for seamless scheduling, solid supervision for ongoing professional growth, clear therapy contracts and policies in place to set the stage for a successful therapeutic relationship.

Payment procedures established, comprehensive assessments and documentation templates and preparing clients with essential materials play pivotal roles in each step of the therapeutic process. We'll discuss the mechanics of these components, offering practical strategies so you can easily manage them.

The preparations you now make pave the way for the therapeutic journey ahead and set the stage for enjoying your private practice, feeling confident and in control and ensuring clients have a positive experience and can benefit from the effective therapy you deliver. When a business is running smoothly, it enhances the therapeutic alliance and honours the responsibility we hold as therapists in business.

Creating Your Ideal Week

Let's begin with a fundamental element: setting clear work/life boundaries. These boundaries will define the scope of your practice and inform the shape of your professional week. Seeing clients and delivering therapy is very much in our comfort zone. Therefore, we can quickly find ourselves going all in, seeing clients, being busy with our clinical work and forgetting we are actually wearing two hats, one as a therapist and the other as a business owner. Therefore, spend some time

DOI: 10.4324/9781003401391-9

WORKING WEEK

	Mon	Tue	Wed	Thu	Fri	Sat	Sun
07:00							
08:00							
09:00							
10:00							
11:00							
12:00							
13:00							
14:00							
15:00							
16:00							
17:00							
18.00							
19.00							
20.00							
21.00							
22.00							

Figure 8.1 Working week.

planning and ensuring you balance delivering clinical work and running your business sustainably. You need to intentionally design your weekly schedule in a way that works for you and allows you to thrive personally and professionally, establishing clear boundaries between your work and personal life. Doing so will help you avoid burnout and overwhelm, which can quickly creep up on us without the boundaries of a 9–5 job.

Your first step is to decide on your working hours. Initially, it can be tempting to work as and when your clients can see you, but as you get busier, this will soon become unsustainable, so set boundaries early on to avoid this; starting with the end in mind will stand you in good stead.

Plan out when your working day will start and finish and when you will take lunch breaks, using the template provided in Figure 8.1. This enables you to see the client appointments available each day.

Ensure you have enough time between clients to recharge, write your notes, do the invoicing and prepare for the next session. Set realistic limits on the number of clients you can see per day or week and allow some buffer time for unexpected tasks like managing a risk situation or writing an unexpected report.

Creating your ideal week is a continuous process of trial and error and adjustment. By intentionally designing your schedule to align with your values and goals, you'll achieve a harmonious balance that allows you to excel as a therapist and live a fulfilling life outside of work. I review my ideal week every quarter and spend an hour reviewing my business.

Time Management

Even with your ideal week in place, we can still find ourselves forgetting to come up for air, and before we know it, our working week is a non-stop whirlwind of therapy sessions and paperwork. It's an easy trap to fall into; the antidote is in the systems you put in place for your business from the very start, which will support you in the planning and prioritising of your workload, keeping your focus laser-sharp. Here are a few strategies to consider:

- *Time blocking:* Allocate specific blocks of time for different tasks, such as client sessions, administrative work, note writing, marketing and self-care. This maintains focus and prevents overlapping responsibilities.
- *Expectations:* Be realistic about how much you can accomplish within a given time frame. Avoid overcommitting or taking on more clients than you can comfortably handle.
- *Delegate and outsource:* Identify tasks that can be delegated or outsourced to free up your time and focus on your core responsibilities. This could include hiring an administrative assistant, outsourcing billing and insurance tasks or seeking marketing support.
- *Buffer time:* Allow buffer time between client sessions or tasks to recharge, reflect and transition smoothly.
- *Use technology:* Explore time management and productivity tools that can help streamline your workflow and keep you organised. Calendar apps, project management software and task-tracking tools can assist in managing your schedule and priorities effectively.

Good time management strategies are like sturdy foundations that will keep you grounded and focused and help you make the most of your week.

Supervision and Support

Your next foundational pillar is establishing a robust support network around yourself and your practice. Clinical supervision is the backbone of this support, providing you with guidance, perspective and a safeguard for both you and your clients. I often recommend having two supervisors in case one is on annual leave or just to have additional support and a different perspective. Consider finding a supervisor who's also experienced in private practice and shares a similar or complementary approach to enrich your professional support with diverse insights and reflective opportunities.

As part of the supervision agreement, which lays out the expectations and boundaries of the supervisory relationship, discuss any out-of-hours support they can provide or what to do if you have concerns or a crisis or need support outside of the supervision arrangement. Are they happy to support you in managing your therapeutic/clinical will or overall practice and career goals? You can quickly see that you need various people to support you. Beyond the one-on-one supervision, consider the collective wisdom offered by peer supervision groups. These groups are not only cost-effective but serve as a crucible for sharing experiences, strategies and support with colleagues who are navigating similar professional paths. Being attuned to the shared challenges and victories of peers can be incredibly reaffirming and grounding. Or you could work with a business coach alongside having clinical support.

Finally, ensure you know all the numbers and contact details of the local services that could be essential for your clients. Knowing whom to call upon when a client's needs extend beyond your practice's scope is not just good practice; it's an ethical imperative. From mental health crisis teams to specialised community resources, being knowledgeable about local services ensures you can provide comprehensive care by referring or collaborating when necessary. Building this supportive infrastructure takes time and is as crucial as any other preparation for your therapy sessions. It anchors you in a professional community, supports your practice's ethical and clinical integrity and, ultimately, empowers you to provide the highest level of care to your clients. To ensure the support you have continues to meet your evolving practice needs, regularly review each support system in place.

Therapeutic/Clinical Wills

Before we move on to the practicalities, take a moment to envision the unthinkable. What would the impact be if you could not go to work on Monday? Who would inform your clients, and what would happen to the confidential information held in your private practice if the unexpected were to occur? I'm talking about sudden death, serious illness or incapacitation. Admittedly, it's a rather sad enquiry that most individuals prefer to avoid. Nevertheless, as therapists operating in private practice, we carry the weighty responsibility of upholding professional and ethical obligations towards our clients, necessitating that we establish sufficient provisions for these eventualities. The British Association for Behavioural and Cognitive Psychotherapies (BABCP) has recently introduced instating a clinical will as a professional standard within psychotherapy.

A therapeutic or clinical will is a document detailing the actions needed to either suspend or close your therapy practice in case of your unexpected death or incapacity. At Pocketsite.co.uk, you can download a template or create your own incorporating these elements:

- Support, containment and ethical management of clients in informing them and helping them decide what they want to do next, and how to go about this.
- Terminating ethically and responsibly aspects of the therapist's practice that require client confidentiality to be preserved.

- Overview of financial and administration commitments, associated passwords, access and bank details.
- Outline of procedures involving the closure of your practice, such as insurance, membership of professional bodies, ending of training or writing contracts and tying up financial affairs.

Professional bodies generally require therapists to nominate two qualified therapists to act on a therapist's behalf in the event of incapacity and to carry out the terms of the clinical will.

Ensuring you have a therapeutic will is primarily about protecting the welfare and confidentiality of your clients. It's unlikely you'd have become a therapist in the first place if you didn't care deeply about these things.

Essential Paperwork

Your time is organised, you have a support system in place are prepared for the worst. Next is to get the necessary paperwork in place. Here's an overview of the paperwork that is useful to collate before you see your first client. There is a checklist at the end of the chapter to work your way through.

- Initial contact form
- Therapy agreement
- Therapeutic will
- Assessment documentation
- Notes template
- Risk assessment form
- Consent to share information
- Clinical measures, if required
- Therapy information sheets
- Psychoeducational material
- Assessment forms
- Letterhead
- Invoice template

DBS Checks

Will you have a background check done? Each country has its own legal framework and procedures for conducting such checks, and the requirements may vary depending on the nature of the work and the level of contact with vulnerable populations. It's essential for individuals working internationally or for international organisations to understand and comply with the local regulations regarding background checks; also check with your indemnity insurance that you are covered to work with people in other countries. In the UK, this is called a DBS check. DBS stands for Disclosure and Barring Service. It is a UK government agency responsible for conducting criminal record checks. The purpose of a DBS check is to provide information about an individual's criminal history, helping employers and organisations make informed decisions regarding the suitability of individuals for certain roles, particularly those involving work with vulnerable groups, such as children or adults at risk. It aims to promote safer recruitment practices and protect the well-being of vulnerable populations. This is generally a standard requirement if you work for third parties, and your insurance company may recommend it too.

The DBS or background check reveals spent and unspent convictions, cautions, reprimands and warnings. The need for a DBS check depends on various factors, including the nature of your work and the individuals you serve. While there is no blanket legal obligation for therapists in private practice to undergo a check, it is recommended as therapists often work with vulnerable individuals, and therefore, it demonstrates your commitment to safety and professionalism, reassuring clients and building trust. Consult professional bodies or seek legal advice to understand specific requirements. Background check systems vary by country, so consult relevant authorities for information outside the UK.

Onboarding Clients

Even before someone enquires about having therapy with you, it's helpful to have a page on your website which provides an outline of some of the practicalities, such as the process of how to arrange sessions with you, the days and times you work, your prices, the ways people can pay and how many sessions they may require. This information is often provided on the contact page of a website.

If you have been writing blog posts for your business, it's a nice touch to direct them to some of your work so they can get a feel for what you are like and how you work.

You must set up indemnity insurance before your first client walks in the door. This acts like a safety net, protecting you against legal claims or allegations related to your professional practice. Once set up, ensure you have a reminder in your calendar each year to renew this.

It's now time to book the first appointment. You will need either a diary or a clinical system which can act as a diary, appointment reminder, notes system and invoicing software. While there will be a cost for this, it will save you a lot of time and energy. With the first appointment booked, you have your first client. The next document to have in place is the 'Initial Contact Information.' This would include basic information such as:

- Name
- Address
- Date of birth
- GP information
- Next-of-kin details in case of an emergency
- The days and times that suit them for an appointment
- How they would like to receive therapy (i.e. online or face-to-face)
- An overview of why they would like sessions and their therapy goals

- You can ask them to provide these details if they will be paying through private healthcare
- How did they learn about your practice to understand which areas of your marketing are most effective?

Once your new client has completed the initial documentation, you are then in receipt of sensitive data and need to refer back to Chapter 7 on data protection to ensure you are handling the data appropriately. Therefore, you need to register with the ICO if in the UK and ensure you inform the client how you will store their data and why you require it.

Appointment Reminders

Text and email reminders have been a game-changer for my private practice, as they significantly reduce late cancellations and missed appointments. Setting these up on clinical software platforms have a small charge, but they will save you more in the long run. We all have busy lives and people appreciate receiving a gentle nudge to help them remember appointments.

Therapy Agreement

This has been covered in depth in Chapter 7 on data protection, so for a comprehensive overview of what you need to include, head back and have a read-through. It's worth mentioning again here, as having your therapy agreement in place is essential for getting ready for therapy sessions.

The therapy agreement serves as the understanding between therapist and client, outlining the terms and conditions of the therapy journey. The agreement is essential, whether written or digital; clients have the right to know what to expect in therapy, and the agreement ensures transparency. To create an effective agreement, you can use templates like the one available at Pocketsite.co.uk or write it yourself.

I generally email this to clients when they book their first appointment to ensure they have the information about how I will look after their data. You can then discuss it further and ensure they understand it in the first session when they have had time to read it.

Therapy Environment

These days, therapy delivery has expanded far beyond the traditional therapy room through various mediums such as online video sessions, phone calls, text-based communication and outdoor walking sessions. All these options provide flexibility and accessibility for therapists and their clients alike so that therapy can be delivered in ways that best suit everyone's preferences and circumstances. With the continuous technological advancements, I'm sure the virtual therapy room is on the horizon.

Online therapy has recently gained popularity as a convenient and accessible delivery mode. It offers flexibility and allows individuals to engage in therapy from the comfort of their own homes or any location with an internet connection. The concept of a 'walking therapy room' also grew popular during the pandemic. It combines the benefits of physical movement and nature within the therapeutic process. To translate this concept to online therapy, some therapists encourage clients to participate in video sessions while walking outdoors, separately or together. Some therapists have built beautiful therapy rooms in their gardens or rent local offices.

The numerous ways we can deliver therapy promote accessibility and continuity of care, which is a constantly evolving landscape, especially with the advances of the digital world. In the book *The Digital Delivery of Mental Health Therapies*, Wilson (2022) brings together a wealth of experience, knowledge and skills around utilising digital means of delivering mental health therapies and discusses the importance of keeping up to date with what is available so we can ensure our clients can make informed choices about their care. This text is a comprehensive overview of all the considerations of delivering therapy in the digital age and is worth a read.

In my practice, many clients chose a blended approach to therapy, where I see them online, face-to-face and a mixture of both. This is perfect for students travelling between home and university, new parents who can struggle to get out of the house, and for people who travel for work. Whatever you decide regarding where and how you will deliver your therapy, the key is planning, setting up and discussing with the client how their needs can be best met. It's also important to regularly review the therapeutic environment in which therapy is being delivered.

Creating a therapeutic space, whether physical or digital, is about designing and cultivating an environment that is both reassuring and conducive to well-being. The essentials of such a space include confidentiality, safety and a sense of secure quietude. It's a setting where professional boundaries are clear and strong, designed to nurture the therapeutic process. In this space, the ambience is carefully considered: lighting is soft yet sufficient, seating invites comfort without informality and distractions are pared down to the barest whisper. The placement of furniture and the choice of decor are not by chance; they are deliberate strokes to paint a serene backdrop that encourages relaxation and a readiness to share. Whether sessions are online or in person, these principles hold firm. I used to try to enhance my therapy room with various smells I liked, but I soon found out that what one person likes, another doesn't or could even be allergic to, so I now work on keeping my therapy room neutral smelling and have invested in an air filter that constantly cleans the room's air. So it's neutral, fresh and bug-free, which became important during the recent pandemic.

Maintaining a space for therapy is a deeply intentional act that doesn't waver whether you're sitting across from your client or greeting them through a screen. It's about more than just setting boundaries and guidelines; it's about weaving these into the very fabric of your practice, ensuring they're as much a part of the therapy as the conversation itself, creating a reliable foundation where trust can build, allowing clients to navigate their personal journeys.

During Therapy

The first session is like opening a brand-new book. It starts a journey filled with possibilities and pathways yet to be explored. You might start by putting together a 'Starting Therapy Pack' for clients, including the best way they can contact you and psycho-education information that might be useful for them to read through. The pack can act as an additional communication bridge that guides them gently into the therapeutic process.

I provide information on the therapies I deliver, a building resilience guide with some basic mental health strategies, a notepad and a pen. You could also include clinical measures or basic questionnaires to aid the assessment process. It's also another opportunity to provide an overview of key policies you have in place and inform them of what they can do if they need support out of hours or in an emergency. These packs aren't one-size-fits-all. A nice touch is personalising them to fit each individual's needs.

Assessment

An assessment document is a helpful tool as it acts as a roadmap that guides you through asking the right questions to gather the essential information required to navigate the therapeutic journey ahead. It helps us understand our client's history, struggles and hopes for therapy. It's more than a series of boxes to be ticked. It's the first step towards building a strong therapeutic alliance, demonstrating our commitment to understanding their story and tailoring our approach to each client's unique needs. You may not require a template for assessments, but some therapists like to have this as a guide to ensure they have everything covered.

Typically, an initial assessment involves various components, including a thorough intake interview, gathering relevant personal and medical history, assessing the client's current symptoms and functioning, exploring their social support system, identifying any previous therapy experiences, and conducting appropriate psychological assessments or screenings. Therapists may also enquire about any past or current risks the client may have experienced or be facing. These risks can include factors such as self-harm, substance abuse or traumatic events. Therapists must assess and address these risks to ensure the client's safety and well-being. Further exploration of risk assessment and management will be covered in greater depth in the next chapter.

Additionally, therapists may enquire about the client's expectations, goals, preferences and motivations for seeking therapy, allowing for a more tailored approach to their treatment. This comprehensive assessment enables therapists to develop a personalised treatment plan and work collaboratively with clients towards their desired therapy goals.

If you decide that the client is not the right fit for you at the end of the assessment, then you can discuss this with the client, and then it's common practice to support the client in finding another therapist or accessing a more appropriate service. For example, some people have complex needs better suited to organisations with access to multidisciplinary teams, such as clients with eating disorders. You may feel there's a risk that can't be managed in your practice setting, or the client's presentation may simply be outside your scope of expertise. Knowing where your local services are based and how to access them is useful information to have collated in one place for when you need them.

Notes

After each session, it's time to take notes. Some therapists find it helpful to jot down brief points during the session and flesh them out in more detail afterwards. Others prefer to rely on their memory and write comprehensive notes after the session.

Then comes the question of storage. In this digital age, many opt for electronic note-keeping for its convenience and efficiency. Although there's a cost, I recommend this option for ease and enhanced security. If you choose this route, be sure to select a platform that's not only user-friendly but also prioritises data protection. If you're more of a pen-and-paper person, ensure your physical notes are stored in a secure, locked location in line with data protection regulations.

As there are occasions when you could be asked to share your treatment notes, you will need to discuss this with your client and ask for their consent. For this reason, I recommend having a 'consent to share' information sheet on hand when you begin seeing clients and taking notes.

The document should include details about the purpose of information sharing, the specific information to be shared, how it will be shared and the intended recipients. It's important to outline the client's rights and clearly explain how their privacy will be protected. The consent form may also address any potential risks, benefits or limitations of sharing information. There should be three copies: one for your records, one for the client and one for the data recipient.

Ultimately, you must ensure a clear policy for managing, storing and sharing notes that is reviewed regularly in line with data protection legislation. More detail can be found in Chapter 7, which covers data protection.

Taking Payment

Next, you'll want to choose a payment method that's both convenient for your clients and easy for you to manage. Options may include cash, bank transfer, card payment or digital payments through secure platforms like PayPal. Remember to ensure any method you use maintains the highest level of data security to protect your client's financial information.

Keeping track of payments is also essential. Use secure and reliable accounting software to record payments, generate invoices and receipts and track your income.

This ensures you maintain accurate financial records for tax purposes and lets you stay on top of any outstanding payments.

Finally, think about how you'll ask for payment at the end of the session. To begin with, it might feel uncomfortable. I usually say, 'How would you like to pay for today?' just after we have agreed and booked the next session.

Invoices

With a payment system in place, you then need to create and invoice. An invoice is a document that serves as a formal request for payment issued by the service provider to the client. It outlines the details of a transaction, including the products sold or services delivered, the quantity or duration, the agreed-upon prices, any applicable taxes or discounts and the total amount due. Invoices provide a financial transaction record and serve as a means of requesting payment from the buyer or client. They are essential for maintaining proper accounting records, tracking sales or services provided and facilitating timely payment processing.

Invoices often include:

- Payment terms and instructions on how to make payment, such as bank account information or accepted payment methods
- Contact information for you and the client.
- An invoice number or reference.
- The date.
- A breakdown of the services provided with their costs and the total amount due.
- Payment terms. When does payment need to be made by? You could also include late payment policies.
- Adding your signature can provide a professional touch.

Many reliable software options can create, send and track invoices, making the process easier for you and your clients. Occasionally, clients may request a receipt for their session, sometimes months after finishing therapy. Invoices marked as paid can serve as a receipt.

Policies for Your Private Practice

Clear and concise policies are the hallmark of a trustworthy practice; they offer clarity and transparency and reinforce your unwavering commitment to professionalism and client welfare. I communicate my policies on my website, in therapy agreements, in the email confirming appointments and during a client's first session. Here is what you need to consider having in place:

- *Confidentiality policy:* Outlines how client confidentiality is protected and the limits of confidentiality as mandated by legal and ethical guidelines. It clarifies the circumstances under which confidential information may be disclosed, such as instances of harm to self or others, or when required by law.

- *Informed consent policy:* Informed consent ensures that clients understand the nature of therapy, your approach, potential risks and benefits and their rights as clients. This policy explains the informed consent process and documents the client's agreement to participate in therapy.
- *Cancellation and no-show policy:* Specifies the notice period required for cancellations or rescheduling of appointments and any associated fees for late cancellations or no-shows. It helps you manage your schedule, ensures the availability of appointments and addresses potential financial implications.
- *Payment and fee policy:* Outlines your payment methods, fee structure, accepted insurance plans (if applicable) and any relevant financial agreements or policies. It helps clients understand their financial responsibilities and ensures transparency regarding payment expectations.
- *Scope of practice policy:* Defines your areas of expertise, qualifications and limitations in providing specific types of therapy. It helps clients understand professional boundaries and identifies when referrals may be necessary.
- *Code of ethics policy:* Outlines the ethical principles and standards you uphold in your practice, guiding ethical decision-making and ensuring ethical and responsible care. You can integrate your business values here – maintain integrity, professionalism and a client-centred approach, fostering trust and confidence, providing a strong ethical framework for delivering therapy and promoting client well-being.
- *Safeguarding policy:* Your commitment to protecting the welfare and well-being of vulnerable individuals, including children, adolescents or adults at risk. Outline the process for reporting any concerns or suspicions of abuse, neglect or harm to the appropriate authorities, such as child protective services or adult safeguarding teams. Specify that therapists have a legal and ethical duty to report and clarify that client welfare precedes professional confidentiality.
- *Record keeping and data protection policy:* Outlines your record-keeping practices, the retention period for client records, and the steps taken to ensure the security and privacy of client data in compliance with applicable laws and regulations (see Chapter 7 for more details).
- *Complaint policy:* Explains the procedure for clients who may not be happy with the service or therapy provided and outlines the steps they can take. It might start with asking them to write to you and then provide details of your professional body if they want to take things further. The focus should address how concerns can be raised, the investigation process and how you will work towards a resolution.
- *Termination policy:* The circumstances under which therapy may be terminated by you or the client. It clarifies the process for terminating therapy, including any required notice period and necessary steps to ensure continuity of care or appropriate referrals.
- *Risk assessment and management policy:* The procedures for identifying, assessing and managing potential client well-being risks during therapy. It emphasises your commitment to providing a safe environment and establishes protocols for handling crises or concerns of harm to self or others.

Having these core policies in place helps develop clear expectations and standards for your therapy practice. They promote transparency, protect clients' and therapists' rights and well-being, and contribute to the overall professional and ethical therapeutic environment.

Finishing Sessions

When it comes to ending sessions in private practice, you need to consider a few important aspects. First and foremost, ensure a smooth and thoughtful transition for clients, planning and discussing the termination process in advance so that you can address any concerns. Provide clients with appropriate resources for ongoing support if required and explain how they can get back in touch if they need a booster session at any point or another course of therapy. This is more common in private practice. As life happens and challenges arise, people may turn to you for help if they have worked with you before. This is also the perfect time to ask for feedback through a feedback form, allowing clients to express their thoughts and suggestions on their therapeutic experience. Testimonials from satisfied clients can also be valuable for showcasing the effectiveness of your practice and attracting new clients.

Conclusion

As we wrap up this chapter, it's clear that the intricate dance of preparing for therapy sessions is both an art and a science. We've journeyed through the nuts and bolts of getting ready to see clients from the first enquiry through to discharge. Ensuring you're surviving and thriving as a therapist and savvy business owner, and building a business for a life you love, too. From the solid foundation of an ideal workweek to the final touches of preparing your client with essential materials, each element has been laid out to ensure your practice is robust, resilient and ready for the realities of client care.

Remember, the preparations we make are not merely tasks to check off a list; they are the silent affirmations of our commitment to our clients and to the integrity of our profession. As you move forward, each scheduled appointment, each crafted policy and every considered detail are the threads woven into the tapestry of fulfilling and impactful therapy practice.

You're now equipped with a toolkit designed for efficiency and excellence. A practice where clients step through the door into an environment ripe for healing and growth and where you stand confidently at the helm, guiding the journey with expertise and empathy. So take a moment to acknowledge the groundwork you've laid. With every strategy implemented and each policy put into place, you have set yourself up for success. This isn't just about getting ready for the first session; it's about building a practice that stands the test of time, where each client's story is met with the best you have to offer.

Business Plan Actions

We've created checklists (Figures 8.2–8.4) that bring together what we have covered in this chapter. Once you've ticked everything off, you'll have the key elements to begin seeing clients in your private practice.

SESSION STARTUP CHECKLIST

☐ DECIDE HOW TO TAKE PAYMENT

☐ DIARY

☐ APPOINTMENT REMINDERS

☐ CLINICAL / THERAPEUTIC WILL

☐ COMPLAINTS POLICY

☐ INVOICE TEMPLATE

☐ END OF THERAPY FEEDBACK FORM

☐ A RISK ASSESSMENT AND MANAGEMENT PLAN TEMPLATE

☐ CONSENT TO SHARE INFORMATION FORM

☐ SET UP INDEMNITY INSURANCE

☐ BACKGROUND CHECK/ DBS FOR UK

☐ REGISTER WITH DATA PROTECTION ICO FOR UK

Image 8.2 Session checklist.

PAPERWORK CHECKLIST

☐ INITIAL CONTACT FORM

☐ THERAPY AGREEMENT

☐ THERAPEUTIC WILL

☐ ASSESSMENT DOCUMENTATION

☐ NOTES TEMPLATE

☐ RISK ASSESSMENT FORM

☐ CLINICAL MEASURES, IF REQUIRED

☐ THERAPY INFORMATION SHEETS

☐ PSYCHOEDUCATIONAL MATERIAL

☐ ASSESSMENT FORMS

☐ LETTERHEAD

☐ INVOICE TEMPLATE

Image 8.3 Paperwork checklist.

PAPERWORK CHECKLIST

☐ INITIAL CONTACT FORM

☐ THERAPY AGREEMENT

☐ THERAPEUTIC WILL

☐ ASSESSMENT DOCUMENTATION

☐ NOTES TEMPLATE

☐ RISK ASSESSMENT FORM

☐ CLINICAL MEASURES, IF REQUIRED

☐ THERAPY INFORMATION SHEETS

☐ PSYCHOEDUCATIONAL MATERIAL

☐ ASSESSMENT FORMS

☐ LETTERHEAD

☐ INVOICE TEMPLATE

Image 8.4 Policies checklist.

Chapter 9

Risk in Private Practice

Introduction

As therapists, we are extensively trained in various risk management aspects, a crucial element integral to our daily clinical practice. When working in an organisational setting, part of our responsibility is to familiarise ourselves with the specific policies and procedures of the organisation we work in, know who to talk to about any concerns and ensure our work follows these guidelines.

Transitioning to private practice, however, presents a different scenario. Here, we do not have an organisation's support structure with their guidance framework and policies and procedures for us to follow. Nor do we have the convenience of simply stepping next door to consult with a colleague about a risk-related issue. In the independent realm of private practice, it's up to us to create and adhere to our own set of guidelines and find alternative ways to seek advice and discuss concerns about risk. This shift requires us to apply our risk assessment, planning and management training in new ways, ensuring we maintain the highest standard of care and ethical practice in a more autonomous environment.

Drawing from my experience as a therapist and mental health nurse, I've come to understand that risk assessment and management isn't merely a mandatory chore; it's an essential, continuously evolving skill. This chapter is set out to offer you the foundations for a reliable toolkit for those just embarking on their journey, and for those seasoned in private practice, it aims to broaden your understanding. It's important to remember that everything discussed in this chapter should be integrated with and informed by your regulatory body's relevant legislation, guidelines and professional standards. This ensures that your practice remains compliant and operates at the highest standard of care and responsibility. It is much more than just ticking off legal requirements or avoiding pitfalls.

You must also integrate your guiding values and the invaluable insights gained from your experience, clinical work and the reflection you undertake with your clinical supervisor. This amalgamation will develop your risk assessment and management capabilities.

We will explore various areas where risks can arise, such as the first therapy session, crisis situations, environmental factors, personal and client safety, working

DOI: 10.4324/9781003401391-10

with vulnerable adults and young people, managing social media and staying current with best practices.

It's important to remember that you're not alone in managing these risks. Risk management is a collective responsibility that involves the entire community and service network. There are various services and organisations available for support. Additionally, the clinical and peer support systems you've established in your practice are invaluable resources. By tapping into these networks, you can navigate the complexities of risk with greater confidence and support. Creating a safe, ethical therapeutic environment that prioritises the well-being of clients and practitioners alike.

At the end of this chapter, you'll find a checklist of areas to consider, develop and incorporate into your practice.

What Is Risk?

Let's begin with a definition. Oxford Dictionaries (2021) states that 'risk is the possibility of something bad happening at some time in the future; a situation that could be dangerous or have a bad result.'

Risk can also be described as the likelihood of negative consequences of a particular action, decision or situation. Risks can arise from various sources and involve assessing, understanding and managing potential hazards, then planning and implementing strategies to mitigate or minimise adverse impacts.

One distinctive feature of private practice is that you wear multiple hats. You deliver a therapeutic service and run the entire practice as a business owner. This duality creates a unique set of challenges. Careful planning and ample space and time allocated to this area of your business will establish a robust infrastructure essential to effectively managing the broad spectrum of risks. It will also provide a strong foundation that ensures your own, your clients' and your practice's safety. With this in mind, let's begin to work through the different areas of risk associated with running a private practice.

Independent Working

We often find ourselves working independently, managing schedules and providing therapy sessions without the immediate presence of colleagues or coworkers. One of the benefits of working in private practice is the autonomy to manage your caseload. You will likely have broad variations in the complexity of the clients you work with, and this balance allows you to give more time and space to those who need it, enabling more reflection between sessions and more time to collaborate with others for support.

However, it also presents unique challenges and considerations that warrant careful attention. It is important to acknowledge that working alone can sometimes leave us physically and emotionally vulnerable. Holding this in mind provides a starting point for creating a secure and supportive environment for ourselves and our clients.

The emotional risks for therapists in private practice often stem from work-related stress leading to burnout or when challenging things happen in our personal lives, which can be harder to manage alongside a job that's often emotionally charged. As a therapist, your mind is the tool you use for your work, so it needs much care. The next chapter will explore compassionately caring for ourselves and managing our well-being in greater depth and guide you through creating a self-care plan.

Physical Risks

Wherever you choose to work from, take some time to consider your own personal safety. You might adopt practices such as establishing a check-in system for starting and finishing work, so people know where you are and when to expect you home. Your plan should also cover what to do if things go wrong. This is especially important if you are undertaking home visits, requiring additional assessment beforehand.

Consider allowing someone access to your diary so they know who you are seeing and when in case of an emergency. This is sensitive information, so you would need a data processing agreement in place with whoever has access, as discussed in Chapter 7 on data protection.

Working in an office, you might utilise a personal alarm system and develop emergency protocols around general safety and fire or medical emergencies that could occur. Having well-defined protocols in place means you can respond promptly and effectively in crises, minimising risks and ensuring the safety of yourself and your clients.

As we've discussed, the first few times seeing a new client is a period of particular vulnerability. In private practice, you are often the first healthcare professional to have completed an assessment. This means you may have very little information about your clients until you finish your initial assessment.

Asking clients to complete an initial contact form before their first session, whether this will be face-to-face or online, means you have some fundamental information in place from the start, such as their contact information, address, general practitioner details and next-of-kin information. This will allow you to notify others and access additional support for the client if needed. Very occasionally, clients do not want to provide this sensitive information. They have a right not to, and at this point, you have to decide if you wish to see them or not if you cannot maintain their safety adequately without this information.

Environmental Considerations

Whether you work online, outside, from home or office space, you will be subject to the provisions of the Health and Safety at Work Act 1974, which means you must ensure the health, safety and welfare of yourself, your clients and any other therapists or employees.

Here's how this act applies to therapists. You are legally obligated to assess and manage any health and safety risks associated with your therapy practice, including identifying and evaluating potential hazards, such as trip or fall hazards, unsafe equipment and fire safety. You are also responsible for taking the appropriate steps to mitigate these risks, for example, by putting together fire procedures or having a first aid kit at hand. Also, conducting regular risk assessments to ensure a safe environment for yourself and your clients, maintaining a clean and tidy environment, having a good ergonomic set-up, adequate lighting, ventilation and temperature control. You need to address any structural or maintenance issues that could pose a safety risk and regularly check that any equipment or tools used in your therapy practice are safe, well-maintained and in good working condition.

Consider the welfare and comfort of your clients during therapy sessions. This includes accessibility for individuals with disabilities and mobility issues, through to providing appropriate seating, support and access to facilities such as drinking water or bathroom facilities.

Although there's much to consider, take time to learn about and comply with the Health and Safety at Work Act 1974 to create a safe and enjoyable environment for yourself and your clients.

Home Working

Start by considering whether your home office is suitable for professional consultations in that it provides a safe, comfortable and private space free of hazards. It needs to be somewhere that is quiet and private, where you can prioritise confidentiality and ensure the session cannot be overheard.

Contact your home insurance company and discuss with them using your home as a place of work. They can support you to review your insurance coverage. You may need additional liability insurance to protect yourself and your clients in case of accidents or incidents. Employer liability insurance is also necessary if you employ anyone at your home office.

Using part of your home as business premises could also have tax implications, so you should discuss this with your accountant. Additionally, it's important to communicate with your local authority to determine whether you are liable for paying business rates on your home.

The First Session

In my experience, the trickiest times have been at the first session with a new client. However much information you get beforehand, until you actually sit down with someone and spend an hour talking with them, you cannot fully understand the risk issues. Try to see new clients when others are around, and I would advise you to have more space after every first assessment and ensure they're done during the week within working hours, avoiding the 5 pm Friday slot. Having more time after the first session also allows you to have adequate time to reflect on the information, get support if needed and instigate and plan actions.

The first session is a critical opportunity to establish a foundation for a safe and effective therapeutic relationship. One of the key components of this initial meeting is the screening of risk-related information and developing an action plan to manage any potential difficulties.

Here are some areas to consider:

Gathering Essential Information

Next-of-kin details: If you don't collate this information prior to the session, it's important to get it now. It is a standard procedure crucial for emergency situations and understanding the client's support system. Ask for the next of kin's name, relationship and contact details or emergency contact. Discuss situations that could arise where this might be used, as there could be other people your client would prefer to be contacted.

Medical and mental health history: Understanding a client's medical and mental health background can provide insights into potential risk factors and strengths and resilience that can be utilised. This may also involve discussing any current or past treatments and medications.

Risk assessment: Engage in a straightforward yet sensitive conversation about any immediate risks the client might be facing. This includes discussing any thoughts of self-harm or harm to others, substance abuse, or other behaviours that could indicate a risk. Later in the chapter, we cover creating a risk assessment tool which you can use if you need to go more in-depth.

Develop an Action Plan

Identify potential difficulties: Based on the information gathered, identify any difficulties that might arise during the course of therapy. This could range from emotional distress during sessions to challenges in adhering to treatment plans.

Emergency procedures: Establish clear procedures for emergencies. Make sure the client knows how they can reach out for help in crisis situations and clarify how you will respond if you perceive an immediate risk to their safety.

Client's support network: Explore the client's existing support network and discuss how these resources can be integrated into their care plan. Determine when and how next of kin might be contacted, respecting the client's privacy and autonomy.

Collaboration with other professionals: If necessary, plan for collaboration with other healthcare providers, such as psychiatrists or general practitioners, to ensure a coordinated approach to managing any risks.

Regular review and adjustment: Make it clear that risk assessment and action planning is an ongoing process. Regularly review and adjust the plan as needed, based on the client's progress and any changes in their situation.

Documentation and Confidentiality

Documenting the plan: Thoroughly document all the risk assessment and action plan information and incorporate it into the client's record, ensuring that actions and plans are traceable and can be reviewed in future sessions.

Confidentiality and consent: Be transparent with the client about confidentiality and the circumstances under which confidentiality might need to be broken (e.g. if there is an immediate risk to their safety or the safety of others).

Collaboration plays a key role throughout the therapeutic journey, particularly during the assessment phase, where the foundation of your therapeutic alliance is being built. As you work together with your clients, this collaborative approach strengthens the therapeutic relationship and ensures that each client's individual needs and abilities are respected and catered to from the very beginning. Also, pay attention to your clients' capacity and ability to give informed consent. Here's a quick reminder of the key considerations to keep in mind:

Capacity: Refers to a client's ability to understand and process information necessary to make an informed decision. Capacity is about whether the client has the mental and cognitive ability to comprehend the nature and consequences of their decision. For example, they should be able to understand the risks and benefits of a treatment proposed by a therapist. Assessing capacity is particularly important when working with individuals who may have cognitive impairments or mental health issues or are under the influence of substances. A person must have capacity to give consent.

Consent: This is the act of voluntarily agreeing to a proposed course of action based on adequate information and understanding of that action. In a private practice setting, therapists must obtain consent before beginning any form of treatment or therapy, generally as part of the 'Therapy Agreement.' This means ensuring the client understands the therapy's potential benefits, risks and alternatives. A client can withdraw consent at any time, and it's the therapist's responsibility to check in regularly to ensure that consent remains informed and voluntary.

Implementing a consent and capacity policy in your practice is essential for ensuring ethical and legal compliance, especially when dealing with clients who may have diminished decision-making abilities or are unable to provide informed consent due to cognitive or health or mental health issues. This provides clear guidelines on handling such situations and is governed by legal frameworks that vary by location so check what the guidance is for your country.

When putting together your policies, consider:

Definition and assessment: Define capacity and consent as per your jurisdiction's legal standards and outline the assessment procedures for evaluating a client's capacity.

Documentation: Detail the documentation protocols for assessments and consent and describe the method for obtaining and recording informed consent.

Decision-making support: Establish protocols for assisting clients with decision-making difficulties, involving family or legal guardians appropriately.

Compliance with laws: Ensure the policy aligns with the legal requirements of your location.

Handling incapacity: Set out guidelines for situations where a client lacks the capacity to consent. For example, seeking support or advocacy for the client.

Training and education: Ensure regular training to keep up to date with safeguarding and legal requirements.

Refusal protocols: Outline that you will respect and document a client's refusal or decision to conclude therapy at any point. This is usually added in a therapy agreement.

Professional collaboration: Detail procedures for collaborating with other professionals in complex cases.

Policy review: State the frequency of policy reviews and updates to stay current with laws and best practices.

Ensuring the rights and well-being of your clients are respected and upheld is the cornerstone of ethical practice, particularly for those who may be vulnerable. We will explore working with vulnerability in more detail later in this chapter.

Client Safety

Maintaining client safety is a paramount concern and holds a prominent place in the minds of all healthcare professionals. Throughout my time in private practice, there have only been a handful of times when a client's ability to sustain their safety has been cause for concern. During these moments, preparedness and robust support systems become critical. Fostering a collaborative approach in responding to clients' needs and managing their safety is paramount. This approach ultimately enables us to devise effective plans to ensure client safety. Later in the chapter, I go through the key elements of creating a risk assessment and planning tool to aid you in the process of assessment. Alongside a thorough assessment, having immediate access to the client's general practitioner details is crucial, as it expedites communication and likely offers much-needed support. Equally important is having the contact details of the client's next of kin.

Occasionally, I have written to a general practitioner to inform them of my safety concerns when working with a client. The client would generally give consent for this, but there might be times when maintaining a client's safety has to come first, and it's more important that the information is shared. You always have your clinical supervisor and professional guidelines to support you in making these decisions.

Online working presents the same challenges, but not being in the room with the person means that if you need to get help to them in an emergency, you need to know exactly where they are at every session. Some people travel for work or students can move locations, so you should start a session by taking a location in case of emergency.

Appropriate out-of-hours support is essential to ensure clients' well-being even when the office is closed. One approach is establishing clear communication channels and providing clients with emergency contact information for urgent situations right from the start of therapy sessions; you could put together a list of numbers and resources in a therapy pack for clients. Utilising secure messaging platforms or voicemail services can enable clients to leave non-urgent messages, assuring them that their concerns will be addressed promptly when the practice reopens. Additionally, offering resources like crisis helpline numbers or online mental health support platforms empowers clients to seek immediate assistance. By proactively providing out-of-hours support and safety management plans, clients can feel supported and reassured, fostering a strong therapeutic relationship and a sense of safety throughout their therapeutic journey.

Managing a Crisis

We work with people who are at a difficult time in their lives. Although extremely rare, a crisis could occur during a session, or there could be times when you need to terminate a session if you are concerned or feel unable to maintain the safety of a session. Spend time with your clinical supervisor thinking about any scenarios that could arise so you can develop a plan of action that you feel comfortable with. Every private practice is unique and will require individually tailored plans.

I've had a couple of occasions when I've been assessing a client and it has become apparent they were experiencing a more complicated mental health issue that meant psychological therapy wouldn't be appropriate at the given time. When this happens, I've made the decision not to charge the client but instead refer them to more suitable services. Though it financially impacts the business due to its rarity, I've found it makes the process of deciding not to provide ongoing therapy an easier conversation.

On other occasions, during assessments, I've encountered clients with a problem which hadn't been disclosed in the initial contact information and is out of my skill set. I recognised the need for a specialist therapist or a multidisciplinary team approach and ensured the client received the appropriate self-help material and referred them to the appropriate service or therapist.

These examples demonstrate the need to understand the framework in which you will operate and build on the work you've done in previous chapters, where you will have considered the clients you do work with and those that are out of your scope of competence, or where another more comprehensive service might be more appropriate.

Preparedness is the theme that runs throughout risk management in private practice. Having a list of specialist therapists and services readily available is a valuable resource. When you provide the list to your clients, you're laying out their next steps and minimising risk. Effective planning and preparation are pivotal in identifying, assessing and managing risk in private practice. This proactive approach enables therapists to foresee potential challenges and equips them with strategies to address these issues efficiently.

Working with Vulnerable Adults

A vulnerable adult refers to an individual who, due to their age, disability or other circumstances, is at risk of harm, abuse or exploitation. This term is often used in the context of safeguarding and protection measures to ensure the well-being and safety of individuals who may be more susceptible to harm or unable to protect themselves.

Vulnerable adults can include a wide range of individuals, such as older adults with physical or cognitive impairments, individuals with mental health issues, individuals with learning disabilities, individuals experiencing homelessness or those who rely on others for their care and support. The vulnerability of these individuals can stem from various factors, including physical or mental health limitations, dependency on others, social isolation or limited decision-making capacity. Recognising and addressing the needs and risks faced by vulnerable adults is essential in providing appropriate support, ensuring their rights are protected and preventing abuse, neglect or exploitation. Safeguarding policies and procedures are required to identify and address potential risks to provide necessary support and intervention and promote vulnerable adults' well-being and dignity within various settings. Some professional bodies advise that therapists complete level 3 Adult and Child (if appropriate) Safeguarding Training.

The Care Act (2014) sets the legal foundation for safeguarding adults in England and Wales, focusing on protecting individuals from abuse and neglect while prioritising their well-being in all decision-making processes. This Act guides care providers in delivering personalised, high-quality care, fostering a more effective and responsive care system. As therapists in private practice, staying updated with such legislation is crucial, particularly to ensure the safety and well-being of vulnerable clients. Implementing clear guidelines we can follow in our practice, here are some elements to consider:

- *Establish and maintain clear professional boundaries:* This involves setting expectations regarding the therapeutic relationship, confidentiality and appropriate modes of communication.
- *Obtain informed consent:* Explain the nature and limits of confidentiality and the therapist's duty to report any potential harm to the client or others, as required by law.
- *Conduct thorough assessments:* Understand clients' mental health, emotional and psychological needs. Identifying any potential risk factors or vulnerabilities can help you tailor treatment plans and interventions accordingly.
- *Ongoing evaluation:* Regularly review and reassess clients' progress and safety to ensure that therapy remains effective and appropriate for their needs.
- *Mandatory reporting:* Familiarise yourself with the local laws and regulations related to mandatory reporting of child abuse, elder abuse or harm to oneself or

others. If there is reasonable suspicion of abuse or danger, therapists must report it to the appropriate authorities.

- *Continuous education:* Stay informed about best practices, legal obligations and ethical guidelines related to safeguarding. Participate in ongoing training and professional development to enhance knowledge and skills.
- *Crisis management:* Develop a crisis management plan that outlines steps to take in case of emergencies or when a client is in immediate danger. This may involve having access to emergency contacts and resources.
- *Secure documentation:* Maintain secure and confidential client records, ensuring that sensitive information is protected from unauthorised access. (Refer to Chapter 7 for data protection information and guidance.)
- *Ethical and value-based decision making:* Cultivate a strong ethical and value-based foundation for practice and prioritise clients' best interests when making treatment decisions and well-being decisions.
- *Collaborative approach:* When necessary, collaborate with other healthcare professionals, social services or support networks to provide comprehensive care and address clients' diverse needs.
- *Self-care:* Recognise self-care's importance in maintaining your well-being and effectiveness in helping others.
- *Regular supervision:* Seek regular supervision or consultation with experienced professionals to reflect on and enhance your practice, including matters related to safeguarding.

Sticking to these guidelines and being attentive in your private practice will align you with safeguarding principles and pave the way for a safe and positive experience for your clients.

Working with Young People

The Children Act (1989) is a significant piece of legislation to consider when working with young people. While therapists may not have the same statutory duties as local authorities, the Act sets out important principles and considerations that we should be aware of as therapists:

- *Paramountcy of child's welfare:* We must prioritise the best interests and welfare of the child when providing services. This means considering the child's well-being and needs as the primary focus in all aspects of therapy.
- *Safeguarding and child protection:* The Act establishes the duty to protect children from harm and abuse. Therapists are responsible for being alert to any signs or disclosures of abuse or neglect and taking appropriate action in line with safeguarding procedures. This may involve reporting concerns to the appropriate authorities or engaging in safeguarding processes as required.
- *Consent and parental involvement:* When working with children, therapists must obtain informed consent from both the child (if they have sufficient understanding) and their parents or legal guardians. In cases where there may be conflicts

or disagreements between the child's wishes and parental decisions, therapists should navigate these situations in line with legal and ethical guidelines.

* *Collaboration and information sharing:* Therapists may need to collaborate with other professionals and agencies involved in the child's care, such as social workers or educational professionals. This may include sharing relevant information within legal and confidentiality boundaries to ensure coordinated and practical support for the child.
* *Assessing capacity and understanding:* The Act recognises that children's decision-making capacity may vary depending on age and maturity. Therapists should consider the child's evolving capacity to understand and participate in the therapeutic process, ensuring their involvement is appropriate and informed.
* *Professional judgement and expertise:* Therapists should exercise their professional judgement and expertise to provide appropriate and evidence-based interventions for children. This involves ongoing professional development, adhering to professional codes of ethics and staying informed about current research and best practices in working with children.

Integrating these considerations into our therapy ensures we offer high-quality, ethical and child-focused care to young people and their families. Therapists must stay in the loop with any guidelines or policies related to the Act or set out by our professional bodies.

Creating a Risk Assessment Template

Putting together a comprehensive risk assessment document is fundamental when setting up your private practice. It's also good practice to discuss and review your risk procedures with your clinical supervisor on an annual basis and also discuss any potential developmental training regularly that could enhance your risk assessment skills or knowledge.

When developing a risk assessment template for assessing your client's risk profile, following the best practice guidelines suggested by the Department of Health (2007) is important. These guidelines emphasise that risk management should be collaborative, acknowledging and leveraging the client's strengths.

When I complete a risk assessment plan with a client, I always create three copies: one for my records, one for the client's use and one to send to the client's general practitioner with consent (unless I felt it was important to override this consent due to the level of risk).

The key elements to include are:

* *Client information:* Gather essential client information, such as their name, age, contact details and any relevant background information that may impact the assessment.
* *Risk factors:* Identify and assess various risk factors that may apply to your client's situation. Include factors like self-harm behaviours current or past, history of aggression, substance abuse, history of trauma, suicidal ideation, intent,

planning ideation or behaviours, means and access or any other risks relevant to their mental health.

- *Protective factors:* Consider protective factors, strengths and resilience that could mitigate the identified risks. This may include social support networks, coping skills, access to mental health resources or positive life events.
- *Clinical presentation:* Evaluate the client's current clinical presentation, including symptoms, severity, motivation to engage in therapy and any changes in their mental health state. Assess how these factors may contribute to their overall risk.
- *History and context:* Consider the client's personal history, including any previous mental health treatment, hospitalisations, current support or environmental factors or significant life events that may impact their risk.
- *Support systems:* Consider the availability and effectiveness of the client's support systems, including family, friends, or community resources.
- *Risk-level assessment:* Assign a risk level to the identified risks based on their severity, immediacy and likelihood. Use a standardised rating scale or develop a rating system that aligns with your practice's guidelines. These are tools that have been scientifically validated and are widely used in clinical settings. Examples include the Beck Depression Inventory (BDI) (1961) for depression, the Generalized Anxiety Disorder 7-item (GAD-7) (2006), the scale for anxiety and the PHQ-9 (2001) for depression screening.
- *Establish safety:* Collaborate with the client to develop a safety plan to address the identified risks. This may include strategies for crisis prevention, safety planning, therapy modalities, collaboration with other professionals and coordination of care. Together, you may identify supportive individuals and create a safe toolbox that might include safety plans, things the client needs to remember or do to support themselves, a crisis hotline contact list and information on how to seek immediate professional help such as emergency services or a local crisis team.
- *Confidentiality:* You should explain that confidentiality will be maintained within the codes of ethics and legal requirements. You should also state when confidentiality rules do not apply.
- *Documentation and review:* Document the risk assessment findings and any actions taken based on the assessment. Set a timeline for review and reassessment, considering the client's progress and any changes in their risk status over time (DOH, 2009).

Risk Management Planning

Safety planning is the next critical process following assessment, serving as a proactive measure to ensure client well-being, particularly for those at higher risk. This personalised plan is again collaboratively developed with the client, focusing on identifying warning signs of a crisis, effective coping strategies and accessible support networks. Include key elements such as internal coping techniques, socialisation tactics, a list of useful contacts and organisations who offer support

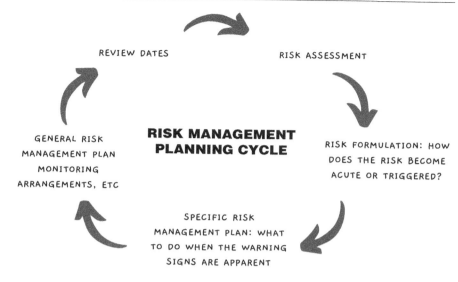

REVIEW DATES

RISK ASSESSMENT

RISK MANAGEMENT PLANNING CYCLE

GENERAL RISK MANAGEMENT PLAN MONITORING ARRANGEMENTS, ETC

RISK FORMULATION: HOW DOES THE RISK BECOME ACUTE OR TRIGGERED?

SPECIFIC RISK MANAGEMENT PLAN: WHAT TO DO WHEN THE WARNING SIGNS ARE APPARENT

Figure 9.1 Risk management planning cycle.

out of hours or for crisis situations and methods for making the client's environment safe. Additionally, incorporate follow-up procedures and regular plan reviews to adapt to the client's evolving needs. Emphasising client strength, empowerment and autonomy, these plans should also respect the individual's unique cultural and personal context. For the therapist, safety planning provides a structured approach to managing client risks and aligns with ethical responsibilities, ensuring a high standard of care and support in private practice settings.

Keeping Up-to-date with Best Practices

Staying current in a dynamic field such as mental health requires regularly updating professional training. It is crucial to keep abreast of research, best practices and the ever-evolving legal and ethical guidelines pertinent to the profession. This involves actively seeking professional growth and development opportunities, such as attending relevant workshops, conferences and training sessions. It is also imperative to have robust crisis response protocols in place to efficiently manage any emergency that may surface during therapy sessions. This means having readily available resources, including emergency contacts, crisis hotlines and local mental health services. With these measures in place, you can ensure you are well-equipped.

Here are some ideas for therapists in private practice to employ to stay up to date:

- *Professional development:* Have a clear training plan to meet continuing professional development needs. Attend relevant workshops, conferences and training programs to access the latest research, treatment modalities and ethical considerations.

- *Professional and regulatory bodies:* Join field-specific organisations and professional bodies to access up-to-date resources, publications and online communities for peer discussions.
- *Journals and publications:* Subscribe to reputable journals in your field to stay informed about emerging trends, evidence-based approaches and case studies.
- *Online resources:* Utilise trusted mental health websites, forums and blogs that offer articles, webinars and guidelines on best practices and ethical considerations.
- *Supervision and consultation:* Regularly supervise or consult with experienced professionals to seek guidance and updates on industry standards.
- *Peer collaboration:* Build relationships with fellow therapists through networking events, peer supervision groups or online communities to share insights and exchange knowledge.

Recognising the fluidity of risk can change – sometimes over very short timescales.

By definition, dynamic factors fluctuate in their contribution to the overall risk. Given the fluidity of risk, only the tools based on structured professional judgement are useful in monitoring change and engagement with the service user and carer.

There should be an established procedure to review risk assessment at regular intervals formally.

(DOH, 2009)

By actively implementing these strategies, therapists can remain informed and up to date on the evolving best practices and ethical guidelines relevant to their private practice.

Social Media

Finally, a note on social media, which is a massive part of our lives these days. For therapists in private practice, it can be a real game-changer. It gives us the chance to grow our professional networks, spread the word about mental health and share useful resources with folks far and wide.

But, like anything else, it's all about balance. We've got to keep our eyes peeled for the pitfalls that social media can bring. The big one? Keeping our clients' information confidential. We have to be extremely careful not to let anything slip through the cracks in our social media presence. And just as important, we need to make sure we keep our professional boundaries nice and clear. This means no blurring lines or accidentally ending up with a double-role relationship with clients.

So, how can we stay on top of this? First off, we need to be switched on about how we behave online. It means avoiding personal chats with clients and keeping things professional, steering clear of any potential conflicts and ensuring we don't end up in a tangle with our online interactions.

Keeping our personal and professional lives separate on social media is important. It helps keep our therapeutic relationships strong and ensures we're protecting our clients' privacy and confidentiality.

Here are some tips to consider:

- *Clear guidelines:* Start with clear guidelines for yourself about what is acceptable to share online and what is not. This helps maintain a professional persona and refrain from posting anything that could infringe on client confidentiality.
- *Moving relationships:* You may build a large social media following and have developed an online friendship with someone who then requests therapy. Discuss these cases in clinical supervision.
- *Separate professional and personal accounts:* This way, you can share relevant information and resources on your professional account while keeping your personal life private.
- *Be mindful of privacy settings:* Ensure your privacy settings are robust. Social media platforms often update their privacy terms, so it's crucial to review your settings regularly.

When we are savvy about social media, we can make the most of its benefits while keeping our therapeutic relationships solid. Social media can be an amazing tool used responsibly to help grow our practice, increase mental health awareness and support more people. Just remember, whatever we do online, we need to make sure it's in the best interest of our clients. Their well-being should always be at the heart of our actions.

Conclusion

In my experience working in private practice for over a decade, risk assessment is an ongoing essential process. While it is crucial to acknowledge the importance of identifying and managing risks, it is equally important to recognise that problems or critical incidents have been rare occurrences in my practice. The purpose of this chapter has been to support you in providing an overview of the practical guidance on risk assessment and management in therapy. By implementing proactive measures and maintaining a commitment to safety, you can create a secure, supportive environment for your clients, ensuring their well-being remains a top priority throughout the therapeutic journey.

Managing risk in private practice requires detailed consideration, preparation, planning and regular reviews of all your practices and procedures whilst ensuring you have adequate support. It isn't a 'set it and forget it' kind of deal. It's more like tending a garden. You need to constantly plan, prepare, review and have a solid support system around you. We are not about ticking legal boxes and avoiding mishaps; we are about striving for improvement and providing the safest service that is possible for the people who choose to work with us, our clients.

This chapter can only provide an overview of the key areas you should consider. It therefore serves as a starting point, designed to help you develop an awareness of the considerations and take the necessary steps to begin the implementation of effective processes and policies within your business. Through careful planning, routine evaluations and reliable support, you'll be equipped to weave a safety net that ensures you and your clients remain secure throughout your private practice journey.

Business Plan Action

Your action is to work through the checklist shown in Figure 9.2. Every practice is unique, but this list provides a good starting point for assessing, planning and managing risks effectively in your private practice. As we've established, preparedness is key!

POLICIES AND RISK ASSESSMENT CHECKLIST

- [ ] ESTABLISH SAFETY PROCEDURES AND PROTOCOLS
- [ ] DEVELOP A LONE WORKING POLICY
- [ ] DEVELOP A FIRE POLICY
- [ ] DEVELOP A POLICY FOR HOME VISITING
- [ ] CONSIDER THE HEALTH AND SAFETY AT WORK ACT 1974 IMPLICATIONS FOR YOUR PRACTICE
- [ ] DEVELOP AN ENVIRONMENTAL SAFETY POLICY
- [ ] COLLATE A RESOURCE OF USEFUL NUMBERS FOR CLIENTS IN A CRISIS OUT OF HOURS
- [ ] DEVELOP AN OUT-OF-HOURS POLICY FOR EMERGENCY SUPPORT
- [ ] DEVELOP A RISK ASSESSMENT TO USE WITH CLIENTS
- [ ] CONDUCT A PERSONAL SAFETY ASSESSMENT
- [ ] PLAN YOUR TRAINING REQUIREMENTS
- [ ] CREATE A SAFETY PLAN TEMPLATE FOR CLIENTS.
- [ ] A RISK REVIEW SCHEDULE FOR EACH CLIENT
- [ ] COLLATE A RESOURCE OF USEFUL SERVICES AND ORGANISATIONS

Figure 9.2 Policies and risk assessment checklist.

Chapter 10

Self-care for Therapists

Introduction

I was in my late 30s when I ventured into private practice. I had a strong sense of good health and rarely took time off work. This was something I had always enjoyed and perhaps taken for granted. I'm embarrassed to say I wasn't great at self-care. My health and well-being had never given me any problems and I'd never learned what good self-care meant for me personally. I know this is slightly shocking for someone who has done so much medical and psychological training! But I'd always felt so resilient. The concept of self-care was for others more than me – until it wasn't. As it turns out, I was in for quite the learning curve.

I was on the cusp of turning 40. I had been in private practice for a few years and felt ready to take on my own therapy room instead of renting from others. I signed a three-year lease on a space where the rent was higher than my mortgage, but I was busy with clients and could cover the costs. It was an exciting time. I had spoiled 29 by worrying about turning 30, which turned out to be a fantastic time, so I didn't want to do the same as I approached turning 40. I was in a good place, running my own business and excited for the coming years. I made big plans for my 40th. Part of my plan was to look great and lose weight, so I began drinking green juice. It was all the rage back then! If you were there, I've probably just triggered a flash-back to the taste! It consisted of cucumber, spinach, celery, lemon and ginger with water. If you replaced a couple of meals a day with this, you would lose weight and feel great. I threw myself at this green bandwagon ahead of a big holiday we had booked for my 40th.

Unfortunately, incorporating green juice into my lifestyle didn't go well. Instead, my weight increased, and I was exhausted and struggling to work. Thus began a two-year journey of discovering I had an underactive thyroid and celiac, a journey made all the more challenging by debilitating fatigue.

In the months following my 40th birthday, I received my free prescriptions-for-life card, a helpful resource, but it felt like an early issuance of an old-age bus pass. A stark reminder of my health challenges. Things took a long time to improve, and on top of this, in your 40s, something called menopause happens, so it was a real party!

DOI: 10.4324/9781003401391-11

Did I have time off work during this time? No, because I was so worried that I might have to stop working, so I worked as much as I could to prepare for the possibility. I hadn't taken out any income protection insurance or had the time to build up a financial buffer in case of this situation because it just hadn't been on my radar!

Why am I telling you all this? Because I want you to learn from my mistakes. I want you to expect the unexpected and learn to look after yourself now before problems arise. It's a common pitfall, isn't it? As therapists, we are so attuned to the needs of others that we can lose sight of our own well-being until it starts to unravel.

This chapter will focus on the importance of self-care for therapists in private practice and the unique challenges they face. It will also provide strategies to overcome these obstacles, fostering a more balanced work environment so you can care for and nurture your physical, emotional and psychological well-being. At the end of the chapter, the business plan action invites you to methodically work through personalised strategies that prioritise your mental and physical well-being in the form of a self-care plan, thereby ensuring that the health of the business owner (you) is treated with the same diligence and strategic planning as the business itself.

We'll look at how self-care fortifies our resilience, prevents burnout and supports healthy client relationships, underlining its transformative influence on our personal and professional lives.

A Value-based Approach to Self-care

Self-care should not be seen as a luxury or an afterthought when we commit to running a values-based business. Instead, it should be an integral part of your professional ethos and daily practice, recognised as a critical factor fuelling your effectiveness and sustainability as a successful private practice therapist.

Having good energy and mental clarity and being emotionally balanced is not just about providing the best service to our clients, but also about committing to a long-term journey of facilitating meaningful, positive client changes. When you prioritise your well-being as a therapist, you are not only attending to your own well-being, but you are also serving as a role model to your clients as you uphold what you discuss in your therapy sessions. You are teaching by example the importance of maintaining mental, emotional, physical and psychological health. Demonstrating self-care in action challenges societal misconceptions that frame it as a luxury or a form of self-indulgence. You are reinforcing that self-care is essential to leading a balanced and fulfilled life. This congruity between personal practice and professional advice makes your professional guidance more meaningful and impactful, further encouraging clients to weave similar practices into their lives.

In a values-driven business, authenticity matters, and our actions should echo our beliefs and the guidance we offer others. It could be said that the attention we devote to our well-being forms the cornerstone of our ability to deliver meaningful and impactful work as therapists in private practice. How we care for ourselves sets the groundwork for the level of care we can provide, genuinely exemplifying the idea that we must first help ourselves to help others.

Private Practice – the Unique Challenges

All therapists and healthcare professionals experience emotional and well-being challenges. After all, our minds are the tool we use for our work. We find ourselves constantly immersed in our clients' emotional distress and struggles, which can lead to overwhelm and emotional fatigue. Experiencing a degree of emotional strain is expected and normal, but left unchecked, it can lead to burnout.

In private practice, additional unique challenges and stressors impact our well-being as we juggle more roles simultaneously. We are constantly working to attract and sustain a steady caseload and ensure financial stability, which can fluctuate, as well as managing the uncertainty you must learn to tolerate when running your business. We don't have the boundaries of imposed working hours, which can mean we work longer hours compared to working in an organisation. We are emotionally more connected to our work when building up a business. As well as a therapist, you are the marketing director, customer services manager and administrator.

Isolation can be another stressor and is undoubtedly a common concern for therapists in private practice. I hadn't appreciated the full value of working in a team and how supportive having a relaxed chat in the coffee room can be. Just a five-minute chat can release built-up stress and frustration of our day, so we don't take it home with us. Unfortunately, valuing community and peer support in organisations is taking a backseat due to the pressures of targets and budgets, but still, there's no denying we have less opportunity for camaraderie, collaboration and spontaneous exchanges of knowledge in private practice. These things can stimulate and fuel professional growth and innovation, so we must work hard to cultivate a community, which we will talk about a little later.

These factors illustrate how the unique demands of being a therapist and running a private practice can impact our well-being and, if left unmanaged, impact us personally and professionally. The antidote is to firmly incorporate self-care as part of your business values and working week.

While I may be preaching to the converted here, I can attest to not applying my knowledge to myself. Despite the comprehensive training we undergo, there needs to be more attention paid to self-care for therapists, especially as we know the impact of working in emotionally challenging environments. We also know that therapists are particularly susceptible to vicarious trauma, where they experience symptoms akin to post-traumatic stress disorder (PTSD) due to being routinely exposed to traumatic stories and experiences.

Understandably, our commitment is centred around helping others navigate their challenges and promoting their personal growth and development. What if we turn some of that compassionate attention to ourselves?

Having laid out the case of self-care for therapists and its significance when managing a values-based practice, we must now focus on actionable strategies.

Every therapist needs a bundle of self-care tactics seamlessly integrated into their professional and personal routines, allowing them to cultivate an environment of well-being that underpins their ability to assist others effectively. It is no longer sufficient just to understand the importance of self-care; we must actively engage in its practice, fortifying our resilience and empowering our continued growth and resilience. Let us explore how to develop a roadmap to better self-care that aligns with our values and safeguards well-being.

Markers to Notice

The first step is to increase our self-awareness just as we do in our work with clients. We are highly skilled at tuning into clients' emotional wavelengths; ideally, we must have the same attunement to our own internal emotional wavelengths. When I was unwell and unsure about what was wrong with me, I thought about how to apply my work to myself and began a journaling practice to get more awareness of my mind and physical health. This was a real turning point for me because I could go back to the health professionals with solid patterns and information, which led to a diagnosis. Once I knew what I was dealing with, I could put what I needed in place.

Journaling taught me that I felt a lot better when I exercised and got more sleep. I'd always been an avid avoider of exercise but having clear evidence in front of me about how it improved things meant I was more determined to build exercise into my lifestyle, instead of staying on the sofa with chocolate and Netflix.

The tool I used later became 'The CBT Journal,' which I sold on my website, and it served as my first additional income stream, making my practice more resilient financially and allowing me to see fewer clients. The next chapter will cover more about adding other revenue streams to your business.

If awareness and attunement serve as the stepping stones for proactive intervention against stress or burnout, let us consider the warning signs we should be tuning into. In my personal journey and my role as a clinical supervisor, I've identified a few common red flags. For instance, feeling an increased sense of detachment or despondency in clinical work and not enjoying seeing clients when it's previously been the highlight. Noticing more self-doubts about professional capabilities and skills. Sometimes, we can notice the emotional detachment in our home life, too, with loved ones. Other signs to look out for are:

- Persistent fatigue, even with enough rest
- Withdrawing from family, friends and colleagues
- Reduced interest in professional development
- Failing to take regularly scheduled breaks
- Noticeable changes in appetite and/or sleep
- Experiencing repeated headaches and/or other physical complaints
- A heightened reliance on substances

- Enjoying work or life less than previously
- Recent experience of life stressors such as illness, personal loss, relationship difficulties or financial problems
- Feeling emotionally exhausted or drained after meeting with specific clients
- Thinking of being elsewhere when working with clients
- Noticing a reduced empathy for clients
- Staring into space or feeling detached or unable to concentrate on work
- Finding yourself easily upset or more emotional than usual

Sometimes we see the signs, but with busy lives and long to-do lists, our own needs still don't find their way to the top of the to-do list. Accountability is the answer to this. Having regular check-ins with a peer or supervisor makes it harder to ignore. Set some accountability anchor points to keep you accountable and encourage more personal reflection on how you feel both in and outside of work. We know how vital and powerful reflection and awareness of the mind is, but are we practising what we preach?

Here are some questions to facilitate self-reflection or to use with your accountability partner:

- Am I setting healthy boundaries? Do I have clear limits on working hours, respond timely to clients in working hours and have regular breaks?
- What are my self-care values? How am I aligned with them?
- How am I feeling today? Work on building a habit of regularly checking in with your own emotional and physical state.
- Am I practising what I preach? We have an extensive toolbox for self-care we recommend to others, such as mindfulness, exercise or sleep hygiene. Are you applying these in your own life?
- Am I taking time to replenish outside of work? Schedule a regular time for relaxation and hobbies that you enjoy.
- Have I got my support system in place? Even therapists need someone to talk to, be it a trusted friend, a business best friend, a family member or your own therapist.
- Am I seeking regular supervision or peer consultation? A space to reflect on my practice and receive feedback and support.
- Am I prioritising physical health? We are learning more and more about the brain-body link and know that regular exercise, a healthy diet, and adequate sleep are essential for mental well-being.
- What plan do I have to deal with secondary or vicarious traumatic stress?

- Am I maintaining ongoing professional development? Continuous learning and development provide fresh perspectives and prevent professional stagnation.
- Is my workload manageable? Overloading can lead to burnout; make sure to balance client loads and administrative tasks.

By asking yourself these questions regularly, you can prioritise your self-care and ensure you remain in the best place for the people you support.

When you're on a plane, they tell you to put on your oxygen mask before helping others. It's the same in real life. We must ensure we're okay before we can care for others. Looking after ourselves isn't selfish. It's smart and helps us better help others.

Plan and Prepare

Prevention is always best. When signs of stress or burnout begin to develop, we must be able to take a step back, reassess our current situation and make the necessary changes in our lives to help us get back on track. The good news is we are in the best possible position to manage stress and avoid burnout because we understand how the mind works and have access to the strategies needed to overcome any blocks or barriers when life happens to us. The first step is to consider the things in your life that nourish and support you in being the best version of yourself and then schedule them in being aware of blocks and resistance so you can work to reduce these barriers.

Earlier, we talked about creating your ideal week. But remember, a jam-packed schedule leaves little room for you. The antidote? Carve out 'white space' or downtime in your diary, specifically for activities that nourish your well-being. Allocate definitive goals and time slots for self-reflection and monitoring your progress. Think of it as an investment in yourself and your mind, your most invaluable tools in private practice.

Consider what a supportive, healthy work environment looks like for you. If being with others is an important value to you and feeling like part of a team, consider how you can incorporate this. I often go to the gym during my lunch break when I work from home and insist on having my nails done during my working week because it feels indulgent, and I also enjoy chatting and catching up with others.

Your strategies for maintaining a healthy work-life balance might look different, but once you know what they are, fix them into your week. You could also add these values into your marketing materials and client conversations, demonstrating that they are not just words but principles and values that guide your practice. At the end of the chapter, I've put together a self-care planning template for you to use or adapt as you need.

Harnessing Digital Connection

We've discussed the need for connection, especially in private practice, where isolation can be a key concern. The good news is that we are firmly in the digital age, which has brought about many possibilities for connection and additional support far beyond geographical boundaries. One example is the Therapists Corner, our community on the platform Substack. Its objective is to reduce the feelings of isolation experienced by therapists in private practice by creating a sense of camaraderie previously only found in teams. It has evolved into a vibrant community, a kind of virtual staff room where therapists can freely exchange ideas, seek feedback and find immediate answers to pressing queries. It's a place where we share ideas, knowledge and experiences that lead to engaging discussions and collaborative problem-solving, fostering an environment of continuous learning and growth for therapists interested in the business side of things. There are many more examples of these types of communities popping up all over the internet. While it may take time to find a place where you feel comfortable and one that fits your interests and needs, it's worth trying on a few for size until you have found the right community.

When therapists join us at Therapist's Corner, they soon find it's more than just an online platform; it's an affirmation that you're not alone. People connect with others, support each other's work and efforts and know where to go for business advice or share a struggle or success story. Beyond immediate support, digital communities foster a culture of continuous learning. Ideas are exchanged, feedback is sought and collective problem-solving is just a post away and the beauty of it all. Geography is no longer a barrier. A therapist from New York can easily connect with one from Sydney, sharing insights and strategies that might have remained confined within their respective regions in a pre-digital era.

When you find your digital community, the impact of such a space is immeasurable. It bolsters self-care, nurtures resilience, and creates an environment where therapists, no matter where they are, can thrive. For professionals like therapists, these digital communities are more than just platforms; they're lifelines, proof that in a world of screens, the human spirit continues to seek, find, and nurture genuine connections. This has proven invaluable for many in navigating the often complex and demanding landscape of private practice. Through shared understanding and collective problem-solving, the therapist's stress is mitigated, and overall well-being is promoted.

The internet is a fantastic tool that's really changed the game for us therapists in private practice. Being a part of Therapist's Corner has shown me just how much we can do with this technology. It's like we're all connected in a big, supportive community, no matter where we are. We've got all these great ways to look after ourselves better and keep on top of our game so we can give our clients the top-notch help they need. It's a win-win, and all thanks to the power of being online.

When Simple Self-care Isn't Enough

I'm a big advocate for therapists going to therapy and think it should be a routine part of what we do at different stages in our careers, even when we are not going through a life crisis. Having the experience of sitting in the other chair is an important reminder of the experience each of our clients has when they come to see us. As therapists sitting in the therapist's chair, we hold a unique vantage point, and it's easy to forget the vulnerability and courage it takes for clients to attend and then open up.

Becoming the 'client' now and then reconnects us with that vulnerability. This experience isn't merely about personal introspection, developing self-awareness and improving our own well-being and professional enhancement. Swapping chairs can magnify our understanding and empathy and, in turn, our capability to reach out and help more effectively. As a therapist, you can also consider yourself a curious investigator of the mind, allowing people to see patterns and make new connections that encourage changes in their lives. This requires therapists to have good cognitive flexibility. Feeling safe and calm is a prerequisite for this. When we feel stressed, overwhelmed or threatened, our thinking narrows, which is unhelpful for exploration and investigation.

Compassion-Focused Therapy (CFT), created by Professor Paul Gilbert, has been a cornerstone, enriching both my practice and personal well-being. CFT guides us to understand our evolutionary legacy and the way we interact with our complex brains. It teaches us that our natural instinct is to turn inward when faced with danger, prioritising self-protection. Conversely, it's in states of safety and connection that our focus can shift outward, enhancing our capacity to support others. This is where we truly excel as therapists.

Cognitive flexibility is critical for therapists, and it is fostered by a foundation of safety and calm. Stress can narrow our thinking, stifling the creativity needed for our explorative work. Embracing the principle of self-care – as the saying goes, 'put your own oxygen mask on first' – is not just advice; it's a professional imperative. Gilbert and Choden (2013) underscore this by asserting that while our mental struggles are often not our fault, we bear the responsibility for addressing them, a tenet that has guided my approach to self-care and therapeutic practice.

CFT's wisdom extends to how we deal with compassion itself. Receiving compassion from others not only supports us emotionally but also reinforces our own capacity for empathy. Gilbert and Choden emphasise the importance of being open to this exchange. It is a reminder that self-compassion and acceptance are as critical as the empathy we extend to others. After all, our struggles with self-compassion reflect the difficulties we have in relating to those same issues in others.

This dual awareness, recognising the need for both self-compassion and openness to others' compassion, forms the heart of CFT. It's about embracing difficulty and finding the motivation, strength, courage and wisdom to overcome it. As Gilbert (2010) suggests, 'it's not only about offering compassion but also about allowing ourselves to fully experience and accept the compassion directed at us.' This reciprocity is the essence of our growth as compassionate beings and effective therapists.

As therapists, we are responsible for looking after ourselves, especially as we are called on to support people during difficult times. There are two humans in the therapy room, and modelling self-compassion to others is an important part of our role.

Practising self-compassion is a way of giving you the edge as a therapist. Just as a musician ensures their instrument is finely tuned before a performance, a therapist must ensure their cognitive and emotional apparatus is in the best possible shape.

In essence, to offer our clients the highest quality of care, sometimes the simplest self-care routines don't cut it. Just as we encourage our clients to seek help, embrace vulnerability and engage in self-improvement, we must be willing to do the same. In doing so, we don't just heal ourselves; we elevate our therapeutic practice to new heights.

Conclusion

As we reflect on the importance of self-care, I want to highlight its crucial role in building a values-based therapy practice. Self-care is an essential ingredient that enables us to be effective, attuned therapists, offering our clients the best well-rested, emotionally stable and fully present version of ourselves. After all, we're not just carrying our own emotional weight. We're also holding space for the emotional burdens of our clients, and that's no small feat.

Through my own journey, I've realised self-care isn't just a nice add-on; it's a protective layer against the burnout that can stealthily creep into our lives. It's a commitment not just to ourselves but to our work and the positive changes we aim to bring about in our clients' lives. When we care for ourselves, we reinforce the values we talk about in our practice. We're making it clear to our clients that it's not just talk. They can see we're walking the walk. In this sense, self-care serves as a reminder that the well-being of a therapist is inextricably tied to the therapeutic outcomes of their clients, underlining the significance of our self-care journey.

Your well-being isn't merely a personal concern; it's a business imperative. After all, your mind is your greatest asset, the very instrument you use to deliver your invaluable services. Therefore, self-care shouldn't be an afterthought, but an integral part of your business plan. This involves weaving it into various aspects of your practice, like your operational roadmap, financial projections and overarching strategic objectives. Working solo in private practice can get lonely and isolating, but we're fortunate to have places like Therapists Corner and similar platforms to connect. These spaces provide clinical support and allow us to discuss the business side of our practice.

We're in this field because we have deep compassion and understanding for others, but let's remember to direct some of that empathy inward. How can we be there for our clients if we're not there for ourselves first?

Business Plan Actions

Your next task is to work through the checklist shown in Figures 10.1–10.3 and create your own self-care plan. Remember, it's not a luxury or an optional indulgence. It's a cornerstone of your professional commitment as a therapist in private practice.

YOUR VALUES-BASED SELF-CARE PLAN 1

- IDENTIFY STRESS SIGNALS ALIGNED WITH YOUR VALUES: LIST SPECIFIC STRESS SIGNALS THAT YOU'VE RECOGNISED IN YOURSELF AND EVALUATE THEM IN THE CONTEXT OF YOUR CORE VALUES. FOR INSTANCE, IF ONE OF YOUR VALUES IS 'EMPATHY,' NOTE IF YOU FEEL INCREASINGLY DETACHED OR DESPONDENT TOWARDS YOUR CLIENTS. THESE ARE YOUR BODY'S SIGNALS TELLING YOU SOMETHING'S NOT RIGHT.

- STRATEGIC GOALS: YOUR STRATEGIC GOALS SHOULD INCLUDE SPECIFIC, MEASURABLE, ACHIEVABLE, RELEVANT, AND TIME-BOUND (SMART) OBJECTIVES RELATED TO SELF-CARE, SUCH AS "ATTEND AT LEAST ONE SELF-CARE WORKSHOP PER QUARTER" OR "ALLOCATE 5% OF ANNUAL REVENUE TOWARDS SELF-CARE ACTIVITIES."

- DEFINE YOUR WELL-BEING GOALS IN LINE WITH YOUR VALUES: WHAT WELL-BEING MEANS TO YOU SHOULD ALIGN WITH YOUR CORE VALUES. SET REALISTIC GOALS THAT ENHANCE YOUR PHYSICAL AND EMOTIONAL WELL-BEING AND ECHO THE VALUES YOU WANT TO EMBODY.

Figure 10.1 Self-care 1 – note your stress signals and goals for self-care.

YOUR VALUES-BASED SELF-CARE PLAN 2

• <u>FINANCIAL PLAN:</u> IN YOUR FINANCIAL PROJECTIONS, INCLUDE A BUDGET ALLOCATION FOR SELF-CARE ACTIVITIES. THIS COULD COVER EXPENSES SUCH AS GYM MEMBERSHIPS, PERSONAL THERAPY, PROFESSIONAL DEVELOPMENT COURSES, OR RELAXATION PRACTICES LIKE YOGA OR MEDITATION.

• <u>CREATE YOUR IDEAL VALUES-BASED WEEK:</u> SET CLEAR BOUNDARIES FOR YOUR WORK AND PERSONAL LIFE TO PREVENT BURNOUT. THIS MIGHT INCLUDE DEFINED WORKING HOURS, REGULAR BREAKS, AND DEDICATED 'OFF' DAYS. UTILISE YOUR DIARY TO DESIGNATE 'WHITE SPACE' FOR SELF-CARE ACTIVITIES THAT RESONATE WITH YOUR VALUES. FOR EXAMPLE:
   ◦ MORNING MINDFULNESS IF ONE OF YOUR VALUES IS 'PRESENCE.'
   ◦ A MIDDAY WALK IN NATURE IF 'CONNECTION' IS IMPORTANT TO YOU
   ◦ AN EVENING SPENT VOLUNTEERING IF 'COMMUNITY SERVICE' ALIGNS WITH YOUR VALUES

• <u>INCORPORATE SOCIAL CONNECTIVITY:</u> IF SOCIAL CONNECTIONS ARE A PART OF YOUR VALUE SYSTEM, FIND WAYS TO INTEGRATE THIS INTO YOUR WEEK. THESE INTERACTIONS SHOULD NOT ONLY BE ENJOYABLE BUT SHOULD ALSO REFLECT WHAT YOU STAND FOR.

Figure 10.2 Self-care 2 – work out your budget for self-care, and plan it into your week.

YOUR VALUES-BASED SELF-CARE PLAN 3

- MONTHLY REVIEW WITH ACCOUNTABILITY: REVIEW YOUR SELF-CARE
  PLAN REGULARLY WITH YOUR CLINICAL SUPERVISOR OR SELF-CARE
  ACCOUNTABILITY PARTNER. THEIR EXTERNAL PERSPECTIVE CAN PROVIDE
  VALUABLE INSIGHTS, AND THEIR ROLE ENSURES YOU'RE ACCOUNTABLE
  FOR YOUR OWN WELL-BEING.

- BE YOUR OWN ADVOCATE: FOLD YOUR SELF-CARE PRACTICES AND VALUES
  INTO YOUR MARKETING MATERIALS AND CLIENT CONVERSATIONS. LET
  YOUR CLIENTS SEE THAT YOUR COMMITMENT TO WELL-BEING IS A LIVED
  PHILOSOPHY, MAKING YOUR PROFESSIONAL GUIDANCE MORE IMPACTFUL.

- ONGOING ADAPTATION: LIFE CHANGES AND YOUR SELF-CARE PLAN
  SHOULD BE FLEXIBLE ENOUGH TO ADAPT. EACH TIME YOU REVIEW YOUR
  PLAN, MAKE ADJUSTMENTS THAT REFLECT ANY NEW INSIGHTS OR
  CHANGING CIRCUMSTANCES.

BY ADHERING TO A SELF-CARE PLAN ROOTED IN YOUR VALUES, YOU SERVE
YOURSELF AND SET AN IMPORTANT EXAMPLE FOR YOUR CLIENTS. THIS
PROACTIVE APPROACH FORTIFIES YOUR PRACTICE, ENRICHES YOUR LIFE, AND
PROVIDES A POTENT MODEL OF SELF-CARE FOR OTHERS TO FOLLOW. YOU
CAN THEN CREATE A SUSTAINABLE PRACTICE THAT PRIORITISES YOUR WELL-
BEING WHILE ENSURING A HIGH LEVEL OF SERVICE FOR YOUR CLIENTS.
REMEMBER, AS A THERAPIST, YOUR WELL-BEING IS ESSENTIAL TO YOUR
WORK; MAINTAINING THIS SHOULD BE A PRIORITY IN YOUR BUSINESS PLAN.
IT BECOMES A THREAD THAT TIES YOUR BUSINESS PLAN TOGETHER,
REINFORCING SELF-CARE'S INTEGRAL ROLE IN YOUR PRIVATE PRACTICE.

Figure 10.3 Self-care 3 – how will you manage and review the plan?

Chapter 11

How to Scale Your Practice

Introduction

What would it look like if you had complete financial freedom and more time to do what you wanted?

If you earned more than you needed and had solid financial resilience for your private practice and life?

Earning beyond your needs and establishing a strong financial foundation for both your personal life and practice isn't a far-off dream. By diversifying your private practice beyond delivering one-on-one therapy, you unlock the doors to many things, such as regular breaks, time for reflection and reading, meaningful self-care and quality moments with your family. Think about the holidays you'd like to take or the training programs you've been eager to book, all enhancing your skills and efficacy as a therapist. This growth doesn't just benefit you; it sets your practice and clinical skills on a path to long-term success, enabling you to touch even more lives along your therapeutic journey.

Many of us are going to spend much longer working than previous generations. Therefore, the work we do has to become more rewarding. In her book *The Multi-Hyphen Method* (2018), Emma Gannon talks about choosing and strategising a plan of attack that gives you the freedom to take on multiple projects rather than being backed into a corner. It's about choosing a lifestyle. Your job title becomes more about who you are, what you're interested in, what pays the bills and what your hobbies are. All these things make up your different 'hyphens.'

At the same time, people are busy and might not have time to attend weekly therapy sessions; they might not feel ready for or have the financial means to access private therapy. Therefore, they might welcome the opportunity to consume mental health information, treatment and support in more diverse ways.

Scaling your private practice holds the potential to transform your business. This chapter will explain the concept of scaling and show you how to build the foundation to do this should you choose.

To be clear, it's not just about growing for the sake of growth. It's about thoughtful, sustainable expansion. By increasing the visibility of your practice today and starting to grow an audience, you will cultivate a pool of potential clients, ensuring that when the time comes for you to offer more than one-on-one therapy, you

DOI: 10.4324/9781003401391-12

have a receptive audience. Diversifying income streams increases your financial stability and opens doors to a more fulfilling and versatile career. Whether you're ready to scale your practice now or simply want to understand the possibilities for the future, this chapter is your gateway to valuable insights that will elevate your practice to new heights. So, let's explore the world of scaling and diversifying and discover how they can enrich your professional journey and the lives of those you serve.

What Is Scaling a Business?

Imagine growing a seed of an idea into a tiny plant and then into a blossoming tree with a strong trunk and many branches. The seed is the vision of your private practice. The trunk is setting up your private practice and creating the foundations in the form of your business strategy. Some of the branches represent having a consistent stream of referring clients. All the other branches are the many ways you could diversify your expertise and skills to offer other services or products to serve people in more diverse ways. Imagine what it would look like if, instead of helping just one person at a time, you could reach out to an entire group or community.

I believe that far too much knowledge and expertise stays hidden behind the therapist's door. This must change because the demand for help far outweighs the available support. Suppose mental health professionals learn to expand the ways they disseminate knowledge. In so doing, this will create a more diverse landscape with improved accessibility.

Trading Time for Money

After a while in private practice, you may begin to feel the wear and tear that comes from relying on a constant stream of referrals to keep your income steady. You might start questioning whether there's a more straightforward approach or just feel the need for a shift. We all value the one-on-one sessions we provide, yet it's crucial to recognise that our capacity to see clients daily is limited. This limitation inevitably sets a ceiling on our earnings if we continue to operate exclusively within the one-on-one model. In essence, you're in a direct trade of your invaluable time for money.

This time-for-money exchange, where your income is tied directly to the hours you work, comes with its challenges. Firstly, it restricts how much you can earn. Secondly, if you are unable to work for any reason, your income halts abruptly. Moreover, it heightens the risk of burnout. Consequently, many therapists in private practice begin to innovate, expand their thinking, and explore ways to diversify their income, stepping away from this linear time-money correlation.

Working one-on-one is demanding and exhausting, requiring therapists to be at their best since they are their business's primary asset. Recall in Chapter 10, where I discuss self-care – what happens if the tool itself breaks or slows down? This was my wake-up call to the concept of scaling a private practice. The daunting realisation that if I'm unable to work, my income ceases, but my bills and mortgage obligations do not, was a pivotal moment. I don't want you to be in this situation, so even if you are not yet, I urge you to consider how your practice might evolve and put some of the foundations in place so you can quickly scale your business if needed. If you never use this, then great, but it could be the insurance that pays out at some point.

We will explore the foundations of scaling a business and some of the practicalities you can put in place now so that in the future if you so choose, you will be ready to take your private practice to the next level and work on those diverse 'branches' otherwise known as additional streams of income.

The Foundations of Scaling

When embarking on the journey to scale a business, the stronger the foundation, the more sustainable the structure, so all the work you have done in the first few chapters will pay dividends now. You have a clear business mission, vision and values system in place, and you know who you want to serve. The next step is to grow an audience when planning to scale. Don't be put off by the thought of building an 'audience.' All this means is a group of people interested in what you are doing who would like to connect with and learn from you or work with you at some point in the future. In other words, it's a potential customer base.

Growing an audience begins with enhancing your visibility, along with your practice. This process involves nurturing the 'Know, Like, Trust' factor and carving out a reputation as a leading expert in your specific area. As you boost your visibility and your audience expands, you're not just enlarging your potential client base; you're also fostering an increase in referrals. This also creates a supportive network of advocates who actively share and recommend your services, further extending your reach. Remember, visibility is key – the more visible you are, the more you're recognised and sought after, propelling your practice to new heights of success and influence.

Visibility

Visibility refers to how well a business, brand or professional is known and recognised by their ideal clients. High visibility means being easily found and prominent, which is especially important in the digital age. It can be achieved through online and offline strategies like social media presence, content marketing, SEO, public relations and networking. For professionals like therapists, it involves being seen as an authority in their field and can lead to attracting new clients and opportunities.

In Chapter 5, we looked at the importance of identifying your niche and crafting an ideal client profile for marketing, so you know who you hope to attract to your private practice. By genuinely understanding your ideal client, you're not just setting the foundation for your private practice caseload; you are also paving the way for audience growth. As you shape each part of your business, envision your ideal client, and keep them in mind. This will then naturally draw in those who resonate with you and who actively seek your expertise and services, fostering a community of loyal followers and clients – aka your audience.

Here are some of the ways you can increase your visibility and build an audience:

Content creation: When you know your ideal client inside and out, you can tailor your content – think blog posts, podcasts, videos, and social media posts that address your client-specific concerns, needs and aspirations. When you create content that resonates, it will be shared, expanding your reach organically.

Engagement and community building: Sometimes, we focus so much on getting more followers that we need to remember about the people already in our community. Instead, focus more on the people following you and liking your work. Create opportunities for meaningful interactions and conversations to foster a sense of community. It's much more rewarding than chasing likes and follows! My coach and Instagram influencer Sara Tasker (2019) says, 'Building a community is initially like being the first on the dance floor; you start all alone and feel silly and a little awkward but slowly, people will come and join you.' Then when people see that you are having a good time, they will join you, creating momentum.

Feedback loop: When you have grown your audience, you can begin to ask for feedback and act upon it. Improvements based on genuine feedback help refine your potential services and offerings and ensure you remain aligned with the evolving needs of your audience.

Consistency and authenticity: When all communication, services and interactions consistently reflect an understanding of your ideal client, it builds trust, which is the cornerstone of any loyal audience.

Over time, the compound effect of your efforts leads to building momentum and cultivating a loyal, engaged audience that grows consistently. More people become aware of your private practice and can benefit from your expertise. As strategy coach Lisa Johnson (2023) states, 'The simplest form of advertising and marketing is making yourself known; nobody can know, like, or trust you if they don't know you exist.' Hence, the visibility of both you and your practice is crucial. This naturally segues into our next topic: identifying the right platforms and strategies to maximise our visibility.

Finding Your Audience

In the wild, the term 'watering hole' serves as a pivotal gathering spot where animals congregate to quench their thirst. This concept mirrors human behaviour. We cluster in specific areas, digital or physical areas, that are driven by our interests or requirements. For therapists aiming to find and connect with their ideal clients, recognising these watering holes and determining which ones your ideal clients use is essential. It's the best way to identify where you should direct your marketing efforts. You can ask the clients you work with already what podcasts they most enjoy, where they hang out online or how they found out about you. When you spot the common themes, you can focus all your efforts in these areas.

Consider platforms like Instagram, LinkedIn, TikTok, Substack, Pinterest, Facebook groups, niche subreddits, online forums related to mental health, specialised blogs, magazines and wellness websites. In the tangible world, venues like local support groups, wellness seminars and topic-specific book clubs can be popular. More than simply identifying these spots, you need to engage and get to know them. As with any ecosystem, these watering holes evolve, so it's important to stay updated.

While many opt for social media as their primary platform, there's an inherent risk as you don't own or control these platforms; they encourage you to put engaging content on their platform constantly so they can sell time and space to advertisers. This is their priority; it's never you or your business. Consequently, you can find yourself trapped on a hamster wheel, churning out content to satisfy an ever-changing algorithm with no assurance that your audience will even see your efforts. It can indeed be an exhausting endeavour.

Tasker (2019) offers a compelling argument for a more sustainable and controlled approach: 'Direct Emails remain the best way to make meaningful contact with your whole audience. Should social media platforms dissolve tomorrow, a mailing list means you can maintain those connections.' This wisdom underscores the importance of establishing your own digital watering hole. A shift in social media algorithms, or the platform's unforeseen shutdown, could erase your hard-won following in an instant. Creating your own website and email list offers a secure communication channel with your audience, sheltered from the capricious nature of social platform algorithms. An unanticipated algorithm update, or worse, the platform's vanishing act, could erase the presence you've painstakingly built. Use social media strategically to funnel your followers to your own online space, culminating in the cultivation of an email list. This isn't just your digital property; it's your assurance of uninterrupted dialogue with your audience. With an email list as your foundation, you ensure that no matter the digital storms that may rage, your voice will always reach your community directly.

Many people focus on creating content and attracting likes or followers, but engagement and collaboration are far more important because this is where you create more meaningful connections. In the book *Traction*, Weinberg and Mares (2015) say, 'It's not just about gaining users or clients; it's about engaging them. An engaged user base is more likely to refer others and stick with your product and services long-term.' So, as we discussed earlier in the book, it's about building relationships, few people focus on this, yet I think it's what we are all craving – more connection.

Email Lists

An email list is a clutter-free direct line to your following/audience. It's such a valuable asset for your business. They do take a long time to build up, so I recommend starting to build your email list from the very beginning of your private practice.

When someone gives you their email and joins your list, they are saying, 'I like what you're doing and I want to hear from you.' This is known as your warm audience, those who know and trust you. A cold audience, on the other hand, doesn't know who you are or is just getting to know you.

Your email list is your inner circle, a personal, direct connection. You can reach out quarterly, monthly or even weekly with informative newsletters, advice and tips, reading recommendations, therapy insights and more. An engaged email list allows consistent communication and builds a community. It's a valuable resource for understanding client needs when launching new products, services or workshops. A warm audience is eager to know more and is often the first to take action.

Earlier, I shared how the pandemic's onset and the subsequent shift to an entirely online practice revealed the true value of my email list. My email list was indispensable when I needed to inform my clients about the change in my business operations and available slots. As the global crisis unfolded, understandably, half of my clients chose to pause their therapy, hesitant to embrace the then-novel concept of online sessions. However, having an email list with thousands of contacts proved to be a lifeline. I reached out, letting them know I was available for sessions, and thankfully, enough people seeking additional support during those challenging times responded, enabling me to sustain my practice. In a world where unpredictability is the only constant and with ever-changing social media algorithms, an email list is a stable, direct and reliable way to connect with your audience.

How It Works

First, you need to decide on an email marketing platform. This is where you will host your email list. There are platforms such as mailerlite.com, flowdesk.co or Drip.com.

Therapists Corner uses Substack. This platform holds our emails, and we retain ownership of all email addresses. It offers the additional advantage of being a blogging platform with an integrated paywall, enabling us to generate income from our blog posts and newsletters. We share many posts for free, but we might create a valuable template or resource that goes with the post and put this behind the paywall for interested people. We also host regular Q&A sessions with our paid subscribers, where we talk all things private practice. The Zoom link for these sessions is also behind the paywall.

Additionally, Substack has a vibrant community (aka a watering hole) free from advertisers and algorithms. As they take a small percentage from your paid subscriptions, it's in Substack's interest for you to do well. They make money only when you do. Although Substack is relatively new, it's quickly evolving and gaining traction. You can create a podcast on the platform and embed videos, and it will likely be able to host online courses in the near future. It's an exciting space where therapists are seeing the income potential.

Why Should People Give You Their Email?

Start to notice when you give your email address online. By paying closer attention to this and identifying what motivates you, you can apply what you learn to your own audience. Generally, it's to be closer to someone you like online or to gain access to a valuable discount or resource. People can hesitate to share their email addresses due to concerns about privacy or receiving unwanted spam. So, it has to be worth their while, and the decision lies in the perceived value.

Many people create what's called a 'lead magnet.' This is a free, valuable offer such as an informative eBook, a discount, an exclusive webinar or a helpful tool or checklist. Think 'five ways to do this,' 'ten ways to do that' or a 'what is?' guide.

You know your niche and who your ideal client is, so it's likely you also know what would be useful and valuable for them. Lead magnets take time to create, but once you have one you can share, it will serve you well. A well-crafted lead magnet demonstrates your expertise and the value you bring, building a relationship based on trust. When people believe what they'll receive in exchange for their email is beneficial, they are more likely to make that trade. When you have your lead magnet, you then need a specific page on your website that's dedicated to it. This is called a landing page. This should provide details about the benefits of the resource and include a straightforward sign-up form. You can then share your landing page on your social platforms so people can download it.

Remember, obtaining an email address isn't just about expanding a list. It's the beginning of a digital relationship, so you need to nurture and look after everyone on your list long after they've signed up.

Here are some ways you can support your email list:

- *Thank-you email:* When someone signs up to be on your email list, send an immediate email thanking them for signing up and downloading the resource. This can also be an opportunity to introduce them to your services or direct them to other resources they might like.
- *Regular updates:* Let your subscribers know they will always have priority and won't miss out on new content, product launches or important announcements. Give updates on your therapy availability or new training you are doing.
- *Exclusive content:* Deliver material that's not available elsewhere. This could be personal insights about what you've been doing in the last month, in-depth articles, share eBooks, tips, or any premium content that isn't accessible generally.
- *Community and engagement:* Foster a sense of community, ask questions and get feedback or hold Q&A sessions just for those on your list.
- *Convenience:* Sending curated content directly into people's inboxes eliminates the need for regular website visits or manual content searches.
- *Privacy and control:* Ensure you align to data protection requirements in keeping emails safe and secure. Also, give subscribers complete control over their subscriptions, including easy opt-out options. I put an unsubscribe at the bottom of every email. This ensures the relationship is consensual and respects the subscriber's preferences.

Diverse Income Streams

We've established that relying solely on one-on-one sessions can be limiting and does not provide the solid, resilient foundation you need in your private practice. You have done the groundwork in creating the foundations for scaling your private practice by increasing your visibility and building an engaged audience. Now you can start thinking about the ways you might like to diversify your income streams. This means exploring the various avenues through which you can expand your earnings by providing more services and strategically widening the scope of your practice to cater to a broader audience and their unique needs. Let me walk you through some of the options.

- *Digital products:* This is an exciting avenue for private practice therapists looking to expand their reach and income. These products, like eBooks, workbooks or short guides, allow us to share our expertise and provide valuable solutions to a broader audience. Whether it's a guide on coping with stress or an in-depth course on relationship building, digital products can cater to specific needs within our niche. The income potential is promising, as these products can be sold repeatedly without the limitations of one-on-one sessions. Plus, they offer flexibility, enabling us to create, sell and manage them on platforms that suit our goals. It's a win-win, providing valuable resources to clients while generating additional income for our practice.
- *Workshops:* Workshops are short training sessions for individuals seeking help who might be looking for something other than therapy. At the same time, they allow therapists to leverage their expertise for a larger audience. You can run workshops for clients or other therapists. These can be delivered in person or online, or you can pre-record and sell the recording.
- *Online courses:* Leverage your expertise further by creating longer training in the form of online courses on therapeutic techniques, self-help strategies or specialised therapy areas.
- *Substack:* This online platform offers therapists in private practice a unique opportunity to monetise their expertise and provide valuable content to a wider audience. Unlike traditional social media platforms, Substack allows you to own your content and audience. This means you can focus on creating valuable resources without the constant pressure of generating content to boost followers or appease algorithms. Therapists can leverage Substack by offering paid subscriptions to their newsletters and content. These subscriptions, often priced affordably, compensate therapists for their time and effort while ensuring the sustainability of their content. By providing exclusive, specialised content to paid subscribers, conducting Q&A sessions or offering behind-the-scenes access, therapists can attract a dedicated audience and create a personalised experience for their followers. While building a substantial income on Substack takes time and consistent effort, it allows therapists to earn additional income while doing what they love and serving their clients innovatively.

- *Renting out your private office space:* If you use a physical location, renting it out when you are not using it makes a lot of financial sense and is a smart income diversification strategy for therapists in private practice. If you have an office that sits unused for portions of the week, you can make the most of this valuable asset. By opening your doors to other therapists or wellness professionals, you generate additional income and foster a collaborative environment within your workspace. It's a win-win situation that bolsters your financial stability and strengthens your professional network.
- *Complementary services:* Consider offering complementary services that align with your expertise, such as consulting, coaching or supervision for fellow therapists. These additional services can bring in extra income while utilising your specialised knowledge in a way that is not as emotionally demanding as providing therapy.
- *Books and publications:* If you enjoy writing, consider authoring books, eBooks or articles related to your field of expertise. Not only can this establish you as an authority in your niche, but it can also generate passive income over time. You can pitch your idea to a publisher or choose to self-publish.
- *Corporate training:* Other environments are starting to understand and value the benefits of learning more about mental health and well-being. You could share your expertise to develop specialised programs tailored to specific client needs, such as stress management and well-being workshops.
- *Speaking engagements:* Public speaking engagements, whether at conferences, schools or community events, can not only generate income but also boost your professional reputation and the visibility of your practice.
- *Associates:* If your practice is thriving and you have more client enquiries than you can handle, consider bringing on associates. They can take on new clients under your practice's brand, giving you a percentage of their session fees. Expanding your service reach and freeing up your time. However, it's crucial to have clear legal agreements in place with these associates. Such agreements should comprehensively cover the scope of their work, the specifics of financial arrangements, confidentiality and ethics adherence, how they will represent your brand, and the duration and terms of contract termination. Also, include a plan for dispute resolution. These detailed agreements ensure a mutual understanding of responsibilities and expectations, maintaining professional standards, protecting your practice and fostering a successful, harmonious partnership that ultimately benefits all parties involved – your practice, the associates and your clients.
- *Membership sites:* These offer therapists a platform to share their expertise through exclusive content and resources. Clients benefit from these digital hubs, accessing support and tools whenever needed. Therapists can monetise this space by offering courses and materials for a recurring fee. Such sites enhance a therapist's income and strengthen their brand, building closer relationships with their audience and establishing them as industry thought leaders. In today's digital age, these sites seamlessly blend a therapist's passion, expertise and entrepreneurial spirit.

As we've established, diversifying income streams increases your financial stability and opens doors to a more fulfilling and versatile career. By exploring these strategies, therapists can create a resilient foundation that supports their clinical work while allowing room for personal and professional growth. Whether you're looking to enhance your practice now or prepare for future possibilities, these income diversification strategies offer a path to financial freedom and expanded horizons in the field of therapy.

Outsourcing

As your private practice grows and scales, recognising the immense value of outsourcing becomes increasingly important. Outsourcing involves delegating specific tasks or projects to external professionals who are experts in those areas, such as social media managers, administrative assistants, copywriters or website designers. This strategy can significantly alter the game, particularly when diversifying your practice either requires skills beyond your expertise or demands more time than you have available.

When considering outsourcing, it's wise to start small. Before committing to someone on a regular basis, I recommend testing the waters with smaller tasks to assess how well you work together. Having support in your private practice isn't just helpful; it's crucial for expansion. Even if you can initially afford only 5–10 hours of help each month, I strongly advise taking this step. It allows time to cultivate a strong working relationship and is much more manageable than hiring someone in a moment of overwhelm. It takes time to learn how to delegate to someone else and to let go of controlling every aspect of your business.

Begin by identifying tasks that consume a significant portion of your time but could be efficiently handled by someone else without sacrificing quality. For example, if your therapy sessions are billed at £100 per hour, and you're considering outsourcing tasks like digital content creation, marketing or administrative duties to someone who charges £30 per hour, you have the potential to not only double your productivity in an hour but also free up more time to focus on your core strengths.

Identifying what tasks to hand over in your business is a critical step in effective delegation and can significantly enhance your practice's efficiency. Here's a structured approach to help you determine what can be outsourced:

Understanding Your Core Competencies

1. *List your daily activities:* Start by making a comprehensive list of daily tasks. Include everything, no matter how small or routine it may seem.
2. *Identify your strengths:* Highlight the tasks that align closely with your skills and strengths – the aspects of your work that you excel at and that directly utilise your professional training and expertise, like conducting therapy sessions or developing treatment plans.

Assessing Time and Value

3. *Time analysis:* For a week or two, track how much time you spend on each task. This will give you a clear picture of where your efforts are concentrated.
4. *Evaluate task value:* Consider the value each task adds to your business. Ask yourself, 'Does this task require my specific expertise, or could it be effectively completed by someone else?'

Deciding What to Delegate

5. *High-time, low-skill tasks:* Look for tasks that consume a lot of your time but don't necessarily require your professional expertise. These are prime candidates for delegation. Common examples include administrative duties, scheduling, or basic marketing tasks.
6. *Specialised skills:* Identify tasks that require specialised skills that you may not possess, like website development or advanced digital marketing. These are better handled by professionals in those fields.

Preparing for Delegation

7. *Create clear instructions:* For tasks you decide to delegate, prepare detailed instructions or guidelines. This will help ensure that the work is done according to your standards and expectations.
8. *Choose the right people:* Select individuals or services that are reliable and have a proven track record in the tasks you need assistance with. Consider their experience, their expertise, and their understanding of your industry.

Implementing Delegation

9. *Start small:* Initially, delegate a small number of tasks or a single project. This allows you to gauge the effectiveness of the delegation process and the quality of the work being done.
10. *Feedback and adjustment:* After delegating tasks, seek feedback from both your team and your clients to ensure that the quality of service remains high. Be prepared to make adjustments as needed.

This strategic approach to business growth enables you to diversify and expand your practice effectively, while ensuring the quality of your services remains top-notch. This way, you can continue to offer the best to your clients, maintain the high standards of your practice and also enjoy a better work-life balance, making the investment in outsourcing a smart and beneficial move for the future of your practice.

Conclusion

Scaling and growing your business will ensure it is resilient to weather any storm, and you will encounter storms on your journey. It's not just about growing for the sake of growth, it's about thoughtful, sustainable expansion. For therapists in private practice, relying solely on one-on-one sessions can be limiting and may not provide the financial flexibility desired, while diversifying income streams will give you a more stable and resilient financial foundation. It can also allow you to generate passive income, which is about making money while not actively working or seeing your one-on-one clients. It is an enticing concept for therapists in private practice because one-on-one work is financially limiting and tiring. While it involves substantial effort and dedication to set up initially, it offers the gratification of financial stability and the freedom to enjoy time off without sacrificing income. Whether it's through digital products, investments or building an online presence, therapists can explore passive income opportunities that align with their practice and lifestyle, allowing them to achieve a more balanced and fulfilling career.

Therapists can explore several strategies to expand their income, many of which we have covered in this chapter. In most cases, having a few income streams makes sense because we never know what is around the corner, and keeping all our eggs in one basket does not make for a resilient private practice. It took a pandemic for me to shift half my business online, but I knew the digital era was taking me in that direction. If I'd had my eye on moving my business forward, I might have had some of the groundwork in place.

Having a range of ways clients can work with you is also beneficial for them as it enables them to choose what suits them best. It can also support people in building up to therapy, which can be daunting for many. If someone has purchased a guide from you or attended a mini training, you have provided a space for them to get to know, like and trust you. We all know one of our client's main concerns about attending therapy is whether they will like their therapist. At the same time, one of the main predictors for a positive therapeutic outcome is the quality of the therapeutic alliance. The digital world means people can begin to get to know us way before they ever meet us.

Diversifying the income streams in your practice and scaling your business is not just a smart financial move; it's also an enriching experience that allows you to share your expertise and impact lives on a much larger scale. We are free to do this for our clients and other therapists. In recent years, delivering training and resources for my fellow therapists in private practice has become a rewarding and fulfilling part of running my business.

With a strong foundation, an ever-growing, engaged audience, and a robust direct communication channel, the journey of scaling becomes more navigable, purposeful and rewarding. When we offer our services in a range of ways, we can reclaim our time, and 'extra-time means we are able to grow, learn and be the very best at our jobs' (Gannon, 2018).

Business Plan Actions

Your next task is to work through the checklist shown in Figure 11.1. It covers everything you need to do to build a strong foundation from which to scale your private practice, now or at some point in the future.

BUSINESS PLANNING ACTIONS

STEP 1 – VISIBILITY – WRITE A PLAN TO CREATE MORE VISIBILITY FOR YOU AND YOUR PRACTICE, AND ENSURE YOU CHOOSE WHAT YOU ENJOY AND CAN SUSTAIN.

STEP 2 – WATERING HOLES – LIST OUT AT LEAST FIVE PLACES YOUR AUDIENCE GATHER AND DIRECT YOUR VISABIITLY EFFORTS IN THESE AREAS.

STEP 3 – CREATE YOUR LEAD MAGNET
- WHAT PROBLEM WILL YOUR LEAD MAGNET SOLVE FOR YOUR AUDIENCE?
- WHAT FORMAT WILL YOU DELIVER THIS – VIDEO, FREE GUIDE, CHECKLIST
- PLAN IT OUT AND CREATE IT

STEP 4 – SET UP YOUR EMAIL LIST
- DECIDE ON A PLATFORM TO USE ....
- CREATE A LANDING PAGE ON YOUR WEBSITE WHERE YOU WILL TAKE THE EMAIL ADDRESS
- LINK UP THE LEAD MAGNET WITH YOUR LANDING PAGE
- CREATE A THANK YOU EMAIL FOR WHEN PEOPLE SUBSCRIBE, INCLUDING THE LEAD MAGNET
- DECIDE ON HOW FREQUENTLY YOU WILL EMAIL YOUR LIST

STEP 5 – LIST OUT THE WAYS YOU COULD DIVERSIFY YOUR INCOME.

ANNUALLY REFLECT ON YOUR PROGRESS AND ADJUST AS NECESSARY

Figure 11.1 Scaling your private practice.

Conclusion

As we come to a close, I hope you find yourself equipped with more knowledge, confidence and a sense of excitement for your journey ahead. Starting your private practice might have once seemed daunting, but together, we have navigated the practicalities and complexities and laid a foundation for your success. The key to maintaining this momentum lies in consistent planning, reviewing and adaptation. Your private practice is more than just a business; it's also a reflection of your values, your passion for helping others and your dedication to personal growth. You will create something unique and impactful by aligning your practice with these core principles.

Reflecting back on my journey, I recall the uncertainties, the challenges and the moments of doubt. But I also remember the triumphs, the breakthroughs and the satisfaction of making a real difference in people's lives while working on my own terms. I've never looked back or known anyone else to look back, either. Your journey will have its own ups and downs, but trust in the process and your chosen path. The skills and insights you have as a therapist and that you gained from this book are your compass and guide.

Sometimes, it's easy to forget that as therapists, we are integral members of a far wider community, a global collective of dedicated professionals all working tirelessly towards the common goal of improving the lives of others. Being connected and feeling a sense of belonging within this community is not just beneficial but vital for our well-being. In this expansive network of compassion and expertise, we find colleagues, allies, mentors and friends. When we support each other, share insights, and collaborate, we amplify our individual capabilities exponentially. This synergy fosters innovation, promotes resilience, and leads to a more profound and widespread impact. This community's collective wisdom and strength is a wellspring of inspiration, knowledge and support because, ultimately, we are all on the same mission. Together, we are stronger, more effective, compassionate and better equipped to make the transformative changes we seek in the world. We can find the fortitude to face challenges and the joy and fulfilment that comes from knowing we are part of a greater movement dedicated to healing, care and growth, reducing mental health stigma and increasing access to therapeutic treatments.

DOI: 10.4324/9781003401391-13

As you move forward, keep nurturing you and your practice with the same care and dedication that you offer to your clients. Continue to learn, adapt and grow and allow every challenge to be an opportunity to learn and develop and get better. There's no failing; there's just learning.

The landscape of private therapy practice is ever-evolving, and so are you. Stay open to new ideas, embrace change, and never lose sight of your 'why,' the reason that brought you here in the first place and what lies behind your mission and vision of where you are going.

Building and running a successful private practice is not just about the financial rewards or professional achievements; it's about creating a life that resonates with your deepest values and aspirations and having the freedom to make choices that align with your personal and professional goals.

This is not the end but an exciting beginning, filled with possibilities, opportunities and the promise of a rewarding career that makes a difference in the world. I am excited for you and the journey you are embarking on. I hope I've enabled you to step forward with more confidence, greater resilience and an unwavering commitment to your long-term vision and values. I can't wait to learn about the incredible impact you will make.

Thank you for allowing me to be your guide and a part of your journey. Here's to your success, your growth and the countless lives you will touch through your private practice. Never forget the magic you do.

The next steps are yours to take, and we can't wait to hear the stories of the amazing things you will put out into the world, creating more options and diverse choices over how people access their psychological support. Building a better world, one values-based private practice at a time!

References

Bartlett, S. (2023). *The Diary of a CEO: The 33 Laws of Business and Life*. Ebury Edge.

Beck, A. T., Ward, C. H., Mendelson, M., Mock, J., & Erbaugh, J. (1961). An inventory for measuring depression. *Archives of General Psychiatry*, 4(6), 561–571.

Cambridge Business English Dictionary. (2021). Cambridge University Press.

Clear, J. (2018). *Atomic Habits: An Easy & Proven Way to Build Good Habits & Break Bad Ones*. Penguin Random House.

Covey, S. R. (1989). *The Seven Habits of Highly Effective People: Powerful Lessons in Personal Change*. Free Press.

Department of Health. (2007, June 14). *Best Practice in Managing Risk: Principles and Evidence for Best Practice in the Assessment and Management of Risk to Self and Others in Mental Health Services*. (Updated 2009). Her Majesty's Stationery Office.

Dib, A. (2016). *The 1-Page Marketing Plan: Get New Customers, Make More Money, and Stand Out from the Crowd*. Successwise.

Gannon, E. (2018). *The Multi-Hyphen Method*. Hodder & Stoughton.

Gilbert, P. (2010). *Compassion-Focused Therapy*. Routledge.

Gilbert, P., & Choden. (2013). *Mindful Compassion: Using the Power of Mindfulness and Compassion to Transform our Lives*. Robinson.

Great Britain. (2014). *Care Act 2014 (c. 23)*. Her Majesty's Stationery Office.

Housel, M. (2020). *The Psychology of Money: Timeless Lessons on Wealth, Greed, and Happiness*. Harriman House.

Humberstone, F. (2017). *Brand Brilliance: Elevate Your Brand Enchant Your Audience*. Copper Beech Press.

Ireland, K. (2004). *Powerful Inspirations: Eight Lessons that Will Change Your Life*. The Crown Publishing Group; Reprint edition.

Johnson, L. (2023). *Make Money Online*. Yellow Kite.

Kroenke, K., Spitzer, R. L., & Williams, J. B. (2001). The PHQ-9: Validity of a brief depression severity measure. *Journal of General Internal Medicine*, 16(9), 606–613.

Lussier, R. N., & Pfeifer, S. (2001). A crossnational prediction model for business success. *Journal of Small Business Management*, 39(3), 228–239.

Matthew, P. (2018). *The Meaningful Money Handbook: Everything You Need to Know and Everything You Need to Do to Secure Your Financial Future*. Harriman House.

McMullin, T. (2022). *What Works: A Comprehensive Framework to Change the Way We Approach Goal Setting*. Wiley.

Michalowicz, M. (2017). *Profit First: Transform Your Business from a Cash-Eating Monster to a Money-Making Machine*. Portfolio.

Moya, H. (2024). *The CBT Career Guide, Becoming and Developing as a CBT Therapist*. Pavilion.

NHS. (2019b). *Children and Young People: Consent to Treatment*. NHS.

Obama, M. (2016, July). Remarks at the Democratic National Convention. Speech presented at the Democratic National Convention, Philadelphia, PA.

Orman, S. (1997). *The 9 Steps to Financial Freedom: Practical and Spiritual Steps So You Can Stop Worrying*. Currency.

Oxford University Press. (2021). *Entry for Risk*. Oxford English Dictionary.

Portas, M. (2021). *Rebuild, How to do Business Better*. Penguin.

Porterfield, A. (2023). *Two Weeks Notice*. Hay House.

Sincero, J. (2017). *You Are a Badass at Making Money: Master the Mindset of Wealth*. Viking.

Sinek, S. (2009). *Start with Why: How Great Leaders Inspire Everyone to Take Action*. Portfolio/Penguin.

Spitzer, R. L., Kroenke, K., Williams, J. B., & Löwe, B. (2006). A brief measure for assessing generalized anxiety disorder: The GAD-7. *Archives of Internal Medicine*, 166(10), 1092–1097.

Tasker, S. (2019). *Hashtag Authentic*. White Lion Publishing.

United Kingdom. (1989). *The Children Act 1989*. Her Majesty's Stationery Office.

Weinberg, G., & Mares, J. (2015). *Traction: How any Start-up Can Achieve Explosive Customer Growth*. Penguin Group.

Wilson, H. (Ed.). (2022). *Digital Delivery of Mental Health Therapies: A Guide to the Benefits and Challenges and Making It Work*. Jessica Kingsley Publishers.

World Health Organisation. (2011). *Mental Health Atlas 2011*. World Health Organisation.

Index

Note: Page numbers in *italics* indicate figures

For Product Safety Concerns and Information please contact our EU
representative GPSR@taylorandfrancis.com Taylor & Francis Verlag GmbH,
Kaufingerstraße 24, 80331 München, Germany

Printed and bound by CPI Group (UK) Ltd, Croydon, CR0 4YY
08/06/2025
01897002-0019